THE GAMELAN MUSIC
OF
JAVA AND BALI

THE

Gamelan Music

OF

Java and Bali

An Artistic Anomaly
complementary to
Primary Tonal Theoretical Systems

DONALD A. LENTZ

UNIVERSITY OF NEBRASKA PRESS · LINCOLN

48605

Publishers on the Plains

Copyright © 1965 by the University of Nebraska Press
Library of Congress Catalog Card Number 65–10545

Manufactured in the United States of America

Foreword

Considering the repute of the gamelan music of Java and Bali, the material concerning it that is available in a general form for the English-reading musician is surprisingly limited. Most of the written material on gamelan music has been by Western writers. Comparatively little has been forthcoming from Indonesian musicians and scholars, possibly because for them their music and artistic concepts have been based almost entirely on tenuous traditional procedures which have for centuries been handed down through legend, custom, and oral transmission rather than by theoretically formulated principles presented in literary form. For the Westerner, there is also access to printed compositions from centuries past.

One of the earliest to make a definite contribution to gamelan scholarship was Alexander John Ellis, an English acoustician, with his treatise "Musical Scales of Various Nations," which appeared in the *Journal of the Society of Arts* in 1885. This gave an account of Javanese slendro tuning. The Dutch archaeologist Jaap Kunst has possibly had the greatest influence on Western conceptions of Javanese music through his *De Toonkunst von Java*, first published in 1934 and then revised, enlarged, and translated into English in 1949.* He not only presented valuable factual material in voluminous detail but he also sought to present an explanation of the Javanese tonal system by means of theoretical norms, seemingly not accepting the wide range of gamelan pitch fluctuations as being a product of an ingenuous system that might not require the pitch exactness of the more scientifically based theoretical systems of the world. There have been a limited number of other books as well as articles in various periodicals, many of these restricted to specialized areas in the field of musicology and/or developed according to Western standards of thinking. Many of the periodicals are difficult of access to a general reader or musician.

The Gamelan Music of Java and Bali includes both information for the layman reader and technical matters and ideas for consideration by musicians and musicologists. Material is presented which strongly indicates that the

* See *Kunst Jaap*, translated from the Dutch by Emile van Loo (2nd rev. & ent. ed.; The Hague: M. Nijhoff, 1949).

gamelan system is ingenuous and that theoretical tonal norms are not compatible with the observed conditions and practices. The views and information set forth stem mainly from such primary sources as leading Indonesian scholars, musicians, and gamelan makers in line with their accompanying artistic attitudes and from the study of recordings of gamelan music made at village festivals, wayang performances, and other ceremonies. The main theoretical tonal systems of the world, both Eastern and Western, have been included, as well as a brief commentary on the elemental primitive forms of Southeast Asian music in order to provide a basis for clarification through comparison and to point up the ingenuous aspect and the position of the gamelan system in the overall scheme of things musical. This makes the book useful not only to the Westerner but also to the English-reading Oriental. Any musician or reader absorbed in his own artistic traditions may have difficulty in orienting himself to a foreign concept. For this reason a chapter entitled "Some Pertinent Attitudes" is added to elucidate this important phase, particularly the aspects that pertain to the music of Java and Bali, and to suggest an approach for intelligent understanding and interpretation. This is overlooked by some musicologists.

Expanded world communication has brought the cultures of this one-time remote region into closer range; it is hoped that this book will give further insight into and understanding of the true art of these beautiful islands.

Conferences with leading musicians and scholars in Java, Bali, Sumatra, and Malaya, supplemented by festival and wayang performances and by generous demonstrations of individual groups, were a fruitful source for the material and views set forth in this book. Their generosity and that of gamelan producers in contributing ideas and information, and their kindness in permitting me to record individual instruments as well as the actual performances by entire ensembles, were most productive and gratifying. It is impossible to acknowledge all who contributed, but I wish to express my gratitude and thanks to all and to the following in particular:

Ki Sindoesawarno, Guru Konservatori
    Kerawitan Indonesia, Kapatihan, Surakarta, Java
    Kepala Inspeksi Kebudajaan
    Djawa Tengal, Semarang, Java

IG. B. N. Pandji, Kantor Konservatori
    Karawitan Indonesia, Djurusan, Bali

C. Harajaroitsrato, Konservatori Tari Indonesia
    Ledok gondomanan, Jogjakarta, Java

Sudharnoto, Chief Music Section, Radio Republic Indonesia
    Jakarta, Java

Foreword

Soekiman, Penimpin Seni Djawa Studio
  Jakarta, Java

Murtadza Za ba, Director, Department of Broadcasting
  Kuala Lumpur, Federation of Malaya

A grant by the Woods Foundation was a valuable conducement for this research, for which I am most grateful.

Contents

List of Charts

THE GAMELAN MUSIC

OF

JAVA AND BALI

CHAPTER I

Prelude

A subtle interrelationship exists in the arts of the Orient, due in general to the gradual impregnation of the various cultures of Asia, both primitive and advanced, by the potency of the cultures of India and China from ancient eras onward. These two venerably great civilizations permeated sometimes gently, sometimes violently, through expansionist or migratory movements, through traders, through religious influence, through scholars. Not only were customs and commercial aspects infused, but more specifically the crafts, the arts, the aesthetic and religious, and more finely the music, the dance, the drama, the literature, the sculpture, which were all frequently bonded into a combined expression of the religious, the ethical.

The impress of the Chinese and Indian cultures resulted in many diversified tangents and offshoots of varying strength in the many regions of the Orient. In some areas the nature of a synthesis with one or both occurred in varying degrees, with the local phase either being elevated to a higher plane or it in turn causing a deterioration of the imported through fragmentation or through distortion into superstition. In a few regions, such as in Bali and Java, there was an adaptation into the indigenous. In Bali a fusion, particularly with Hinduism, of such strength took place that it is still strongly and actively in existence. Here the Hinduism was not really assimilated, as the Hindus and Chinese did the cultures of their invaders, but rather it was adapted to their distinctively communal life with its overlay of intuitive, animistic thought and ancestor worship. In Java the adaptation took on a somewhat different character, and though Java is Moslem today, outcroppings, particularly of the Hindu, remain, perhaps most noticeably in the arts.

Hinduism dominated the cultures of Bali and Java from about the first century A.D. until the thirteenth century. It was especially puissant during the powerful Srivijaya and Majapahit empires of the seventh and twelfth centuries. The spectacular Borobudor temple near Jogjakarta in central Java and the numerous tjandis [1] throughout the island reflect this influence and the state of development prior to the Islamic ascendancy, which began in the thirteenth century, and the Dutch commercial control, which started in the sixteenth century.

1. Tjandis: Hindu and Buddhist monuments in Java.

3

The Gamelan Music of Java and Bali

The study of the gamelan music of Java and Bali was undertaken with a foreknowledge of Indian and Chinese music. It was logical to assume that it would show strong traces of either Hindu or Chinese influence, or of both, since Oriental music is generally correlated with the other arts. Instead, the study of gamelan music revealed a unique and characteristic concept, with little or no affinity to the traditional Raga theory of India or the Cyclic Pentatonic scales of China. The two latter, whose origins are rooted in antiquity, are the great but contrasting theoretical systems of the Orient. Their influence throughout the Eastern world has been so considerable that in only a few places outside that of the more isolated primitive does music fail to show marked qualities from either or both. The Westerner, instilled in arbitrary Tempered intonation with predominantly harmonic tonal texture, needs much orientation to assimilate, hear, and appreciate the sound of the natural acoustical intervals of either of these systems, with their capacity for exquisite melodic continuity and nuance and with their absence of or minimum usage of harmonic sounds. The ever present drone with its suggested overtones, characteristic of most modal forms, and the stratified rhythmic format, even though of scarcely determinant pitch, at times give an illusion of vertical sound. To comprehend these systems the Westerner must divest himself of an enslavement to Western tenets and concepts, particularly in the arts and the other fields into which they extend, and open himself to what are often unfamiliar vistas and different dimensions. These horizons will give an immeasurably broader scope to his own aesthetics.

The term "gamelan," synonomous with the term "orchestra" of the Western world, is the name of an ensemble of instruments which comprise idiophones,[2] drums, flutes, and occasionally strings, especially the rebab[3] and kechapi.[4] The number of performers in a gamelan may vary from three to twenty-four players. The characteristic sound is that of the idiophones and ranges in texture from the thin, metallic tinkles of the high-pitched idiophones to the booming, convoluted resonance of the large gongs. The overall effect of a large gamelan group is that of a tonal stratification of engaging beauty.

Historically[5] the gamelan predates the Hindu-Buddhist encroachment into

2. Idiophone: an instrument with a series of bars, plates, or kettles of fixed pitch which produce a musical sound when beaten with a mallet; also includes gongs.

3. Rebab: two-stringed Arabic instrument introduced by the Moslems.

4. Kechapi: eighteen-stringed, very old Sundanese instrument.

5. The Western conception of a continuous historical sequence of dates has never been a part of Oriental thinking. Important events, dynasties, etc., without regard to dates, are the guideposts for reckoning of time of past events. This is especially true in Java and Bali. Not until incursions by Moslems, Portuguese, Dutch, and others has there been any definiteness as to sequence of time *and* event.

Java and Bali. Its present form has apparently changed little in the last eight or nine hundred years.[6] In spite of the strong Indian influence on the islands for such a long period of time, surprisingly little of Hindu musical theory or practice is noted in the technical aspect of the music of the gamelan. About the only obvious suggestion of Hindu influence is in the Javanese manner of singing, in which there is an illusion of indefiniteness of pitch on subordinate tones and also an ornamentation on particular principal tones which hints at the gamalkas (embellishments) of Indian music. Gamelan music has been and remains an important, primarily indigenous factor in the culture of these islands, where art, music, dance, and religion are such vital forces in the everyday life of the large masses of people.

In Bali the gamelans are basically a product of the people and villages. They are a part of each village festival and ceremonial, and of the rice farmer's life. As this is an island of plentiful, tropical lushness, where food is easily produced if nature is cooperative, there is time for the creative artistic activity, mainly on a communal basis, with which the life of the people abounds. At evening in the small villages it is common to hear the gamelan being played by the rice farmers and villagers. Almost everyone can play the instruments, and most of the girls can do the traditional dances that are part of nearly every gamelan performance. There are few professional or specialized musicians in Bali except for occasional teachers, such as at the University in Den Pesar. The tonally matched instruments of each gamelan are owned by the village, not by individuals. The sound and scale pitches vary from gamelan to gamelan, which creates a charming uniqueness and individualism. The pitches of the scale tones of a particular gamelan are approximately the same, but the pitches of the scale tones of a gamelan in the next village could be very different. This may be partly accounted for by the fact that each gamelan is hand-produced as a unit by a local artisan group rather than particular instruments being mass-produced for wide distribution. Also, imitation is a prime factor in choice of tones for instruments. If some village (or a sultanate in Java) had an outstanding or pleasing gamelan, craftsmen from other areas tried to approximate it when building one for their community. Ki Sindoesawarno, an intelligent and dedicated Indonesian musical scholar who is Director of the Konservatori Karawitan Indonesia at

---

6. The Embassy of the Republic of Indonesia, *Bulletin for National Museum of Canada* (Ottawa: April, 1961), p. 2, states:

A brief glimpse of its history shows that the gamelan pre-dates the arrival of the Hindus in our country, which took place during the first century of the Christian era. The instruments were then, naturally, in their primitive stage and developed through evolution into their present form during the Madjapahit Empire, sometime around the 11th century.

Surakarta, Java, threw further light on this pitch diversity between gamelans by saying that the nem, or beginning tone of the scale, is the highest tone the voice can produce without energy. This accounts for the fact that nem is not a fixed pitch but varies with each gamelan maker according to his vocal range. This feature was also encountered in India, where the pitch of the Sa, or beginning tone, was flexible, dependent on the performer's vocal condition. Such methods naturally lead to considerable diversity.

During the Balinese New Year, festivals honoring aspects of traditional religions are held throughout Bali in different villages on different nights. A great effusion of artistic expression is connected with these festivals. Since the gamelan music is an integral part, this period offers a rich opportunity to hear, compare, and record many gamelans. The evidence of Hindu influence in Balinese culture is especially manifest at these New Year festivals and ceremonials held in front of the outer temple gate[7] at temples in each of the many villages. The festivals usually start around midnight and do not end until dawn. The large, responsive audiences of both adults and children sit about on the ground for the long productions, in which the performers are the rice farmers and members of the village. The themes and texts for most of these festival productions are drawn from the intellectualized Mahabharata,[8] or from episodes of the Ramayana[9] with its highly intuitive essence, or the Panji Cycle[10] with its more locally centered historical allusions, or from the more mythically based Lakons (texts).

7. Temple gate: a Balinese temple is not a roofed, closed-in structure, but consists usually of two or three walled-in courtyards accessible by high, narrow gates. The outer gate is open at the top, but the top of the inner gates is solidly arched over. Occasionally a few small buildings for various purposes, such as housing for the gamelan or for the signal drum (kulkul), are found in the courtyards.

8. Radhakrishnan, *Indian Philosophy* (2nd ed.; London: George Allen & Unwin Ltd., 1929), p. 481, says:

> Containing within itself productions of different dates and authorship, [it] has become a miscellaneous encyclopedia of history and mythology, politics, law, theology and philosophy. We do not know exactly when it was composed. . . . It is not wrong to say that the bulk of the work has remained the same from 500 B.C. up till the present day.

9. Ramayana: Hindu epic work of intuitive thought, not of the miscellaneous nature of the Mahabharata but dealing with the hero Rama, a reincarnation of Vishnu, whose purpose on earth was for the repression of wrong and promulgation of virtue. Its 43,000 couplets also tell of the wars of the Aryans and the then natives of India. It is thought to be of a later date than the Mahabharata.

In the minds of the Javanese and Balinese, the scenes of these two Indian epics have been metamorphosed into those of their own country.

10. Panji Cycle: goes back to historical, legendary heroes and events of Java and Bali, especially at the time of the powerful Hindu-Javanese kingdoms of seventh to thirteenth centuries.

Prelude

The ketchak performances are excellent examples of the synthesis of Hinduism with Balinese. The ketchak, performed at night by a group of forty to fifty men seated in concentric circles three and four deep around a dim oil light, blends episodes from the Ramayana, enacted by a separate cast within the circle of men, with a pre-Hindu, traditional ceremonial incantation that approaches animism to a high degree. The rapid, incessant, rhythmic chant of "Chak-Chak-Ket-Chak" by the men in the circle, synchronized with undulating movements of their bare torsos and arms, had a supersensory, hypnotic quality; yet it was compatible with the ornately robed characters portraying the Hindu countertheme.

A distinctively traditive form of Balinese theater that uses the gamelan as a supporting element in the expression of mood and pace is the ardja. This form of Balinese drama is mostly devoted to stories of events involving kings and queens. The actors portraying such characters are dressed in classical costumes of flowered headdresses and brocaded robes and appear on an improvised stage set up next to a temple. At an ardja presentation one becomes even more aware of the language complexities common within each of the countries of the Orient. In ardja, if the poetic utterances of the nobles, spoken in the stylized language of the theater (usually "high" Balinese or Javanese), is not understood by the people in the audience, the gist of the story can be gathered by listening to the retainers who shadow the royal characters, mimicking their actions in a cruder, sometimes comic fashion, and speaking the lines in the common language of the area.

However, the gamelans of Bali are more frequently used for human dancers. On this island there is a host of dance styles, primarily religious in origin. Many are traditional without alteration; some are rearrangements of the old; and others are of recent origin but retain certain traditionary mudras (gestures) and aesthetic principles. Because of the close link to the dance, the gamelan sound in Bali tends to be brilliant and rhythmic, with a considerable range of dynamic levels to aid and complement the actions of the dancers. This seems especially predominant in northern Bali. In the southern part of the island, the style tends to be a bit more conservative. In performances of the dance larger gamelans are used, while in performances where the text is more important, as in the ardja, small gamelans, including only about five or six players, are utilized.

As an example of the close relationship of music and dance in Bali, particularly in the attitudes of the dancers and musicians, a significant incident occurred in Den Pesar. IG. B. N. Pandjit, Pemimpin Konservatori Karawitan Indonesia, Djurusan, Bali, had assembled a fine gamelan group of about twenty players and many dancers for a most generous demonstration of particular musical theories and practices, and also of the traditional

7

dances that were complementary to some of the music. At the end of the long day he requested the girl dancers to replace the regular gamelan players, always men; their performance was of a very high order. Conversely, at the village festivals, often the men were seen as gamelan performers one night, and on other nights as dancers.

In Java a different situation exists. With Moslem ascendancy in the thirteenth century the sultanates became the sponsors and maintainers of trained groups of dancers, musicians, and other performers at the kratons or palaces. Today the kraton at Jogjakarta, ruled by a sultan, and that at Surakarta, ruled by a susnan, are regarded as the leading centers of the cultivation of the long existent heritage of gamelan music, wayangs (shadow plays), and traditional dances. There are also theaters in Java that have fine gamelans for accompanying the wayang and dance performances.

The wayangs of both Java and Bali adopt their texts from the same sources: the Ramayana, Mahabharata, Panji Cycle, or legendary lakons, but the presentation of the episodes are distinctly and individually Balinese or Javanese. In Bali they are treated with more religious significance while in Java, which is predominantly Moslem, the religious aspect is less prominent and the ethical, moral, and/or historical are emphasized.

Wayangs in Java, also performed from midnight to dawn, may be of varying forms, such as wayang kulit, in which puppets cut out of perforated leather loom in enlarged reflection onto a white cloth screen (kelir) by means of an oil lamp or torch; or as wayang golek, in which doll-shaped puppets are employed as characters without background of a screen; or as wayang wong, in which humans imitate the movements of puppets and speak their own parts; or as wayang topeng, in which human actors wear masks. The dalang (story-teller), assisted by one or two singers and the gamelan, is the important member of wayang kulit or wayang golek performances. In these the dalang, while narrating the text, at the same time manipulates puppets personifying the particular characters onto a horizontally placed bamboo log in poses suggestive and expressive of the discourse. Along with the moral and ethical teachings latent in the story, there are occasional seemingly improvisatory interspersions by the dalang (or by clowns as in the wayang wong), which at such points often localize the theme or make it currently topical. This has served at times to advance political and social viewpoints of ruling powers, formerly the sultans. Because the words of the text are the essence of the wayang, the dynamic level of the Javanese wayang gamelan is well contained. Soft mallets are used which produce a softly undulating, rarefied tonal color which blends well with the voices and which creates a most pleasing illusion. The wayang gamelan usually has two sets of instruments, one tuned to slendro,[11] the other to pelog.[12] They are used alternately according to the sequential order of the traditional wayang night.

The various forms of wayang are still very popular today. An interesting nonmusical sidelight is the lack of interest in or patronage of Western movies. This was explained by several Indonesians as being due to the fact that the plots were too realistic, too everyday. They feel more subjectively allied to their religious, quasi-historical, or mythical figures as evoked not only in their drama forms but so frequently in their dances, songs, sculpture, and painting.

In the study of the gamelans of Java and Bali, one finds different names in different localities for like or similar instruments.[13] This causes some confusion and obstacles at times. As an aid to help the Westerner better understand the various instrumental types, certain Western musicologists have made a descriptive classification of the different idiophones, in general as follows: (1) a horizontal row of inverted metal kettles played with a beater, an example of which is the bonang (usually in two or three sizes, each an octave apart); (2) an idiophone built with a series of metal bars or plates over bamboo resonators and struck with a mallet, such as the gangsa (gantung, tjalura, djubla and djagogong) of Bali or the gender of Java (also in three sizes, each an octave apart); (3) the instrument with bronze keys placed over a wooden trough resonator, such as the saron; (4) the type using teak or bamboo bars, such as the gambang of Java; and (5) all types of gongs. It is interesting to note that in Sumatra, particularly in the northern part, idiophones are not common. This possibly reflects the strength of the Hindu and later Moslem influences.

Gongs are found in different sizes and pitches. Their purpose is to punctuate or indicate phrase endings and subdivisions. The important ones are the kumpur, kenong, kempul, ageng, suwukan, and others. Drums of different sizes (kendang, bedug), flutes (suling), and certain strings (rebab) are also used, but they are not autochthonous.

An interesting type of instrument called anklung is found in the Sundanese area of Java, and also in Bali. Each instrument is made of two cured bamboo tubes tuned in octaves. The two tubes are mounted in a light bamboo frame and are shaken to produce a dry, quaint sound. An anklung gamelan is comprised of a set of these instruments, each tuned to one of the scale-tones

11. Slendro: five-tone scale. See page 39.

12. Pelog: seven-tone scale. See page 39.

13. Detailed explanation of the individual instruments of gamelans is not given, as this can be found in Jaap Kunst, *Music of Java* (rev. ed.; The Hague: M. Nijhoff, 1934), trans. from the Dutch by Emile van Loo (The Hague: M. Nijhoff, 1949).

of the "mode" used in a particular locality. These were originally folk instruments, but they are now available for purchase in the Western Tempered scale in some of the large cities located on the northwest coast of Java, where they are played by the school children. This is a major departure from the traditional music of Indonesia.

There are many diverse yet congeneric types of gamelans. The largest of the commonly used types in Bali is called the pelegongon. Its size varies, but it frequently employs twenty to twenty-four players. The fundamental sound is that of the idiophones, there being three or sometimes four different size gangsas present. The "cantus" played by these is rhythmically punctuated by gongs and drums and embellished by flutes (sulings) and an occasional rebab. This type of gamelan accompanies performances of Balinese dances such as the legong, barang, mendet, and radjang. The large Javanese counterpart is the gender wayang, which is used in performances of wayang kulit, wayang golek, wayang topeng, and wayang wong. As stated before, this consists of two sets of instruments, one tuned to a seven-tone scale, the other to a five-tone scale.

Chart I shows the range and distribution of tones of the idiophones of a pelegongon gamelan, one made by an artisan and his helpers in a small village near Den Pesar. Many Balinese referred to this gamelan as being characteristic and one of the better sets in Bali. The pitches listed in the chart are only relative Western equivalents and are presented in this manner in order to give a Westerner a primary feeling for the distribution of the tones of the different instruments in the set. It is to be noted that some of the instruments are duplicated in varying sizes in different octaves.

Small gamelans of characteristic makeup are associated with certain communities and their special ceremonial functions. These usually consist of five or six players, or thereabout. A good example is the gamelan djanger of Bali, composed of flute, drums, and gong; or the ardja gamelan, using subdued idiophones, sulings, and drums. Among other small Balinese gamelans are the gong-gedé (older) and gong kebiar (within the last fifty years), which are used for war dances and which have two large drums and cymbals. Although there is little standardization, the tonal quality of the idiophones unites all in a common identity.

Even smaller gamelans of three or four players are found. In Java, particularly in the Sundanese region of western Java, one or two soft idiophones may be combined with a stringed instrument, such as a kechapi or rebab, or sometimes with a percussion instrument or gong along with a singer. In these the vocalist and instruments incline to move in unison, not working independently against each other as in the classic genre of Javanese gamelan.

It must be realized that these comparisons of various types of gamelans

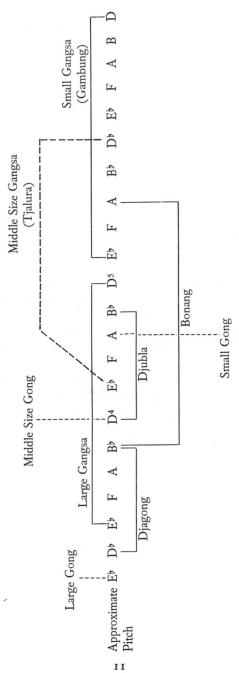

Prelude

CHART I

RANGE AND DISTRIBUTION OF TONES OF THE IDIOPHONES OF A PELEGONGON GAMELAN

To establish the register of the tones, the contra-C, or lowest C on the piano, is considered in this book as C_1 and all the tones in that octave are considered as $C\#_1$, D_1, $D\#_1$, E_1, F_1, $F\#_1$, G_1, $G\#_1$, A_1, $A\#_1$, B_1. The next C is considered as C_2, etc. Middle C on the piano would be C_4.

are being made in the light of the higher forms of Oriental music. In Western music, thematic development and big climaxes are distinguishing traits. These aspects are not as important as such in Eastern forms, which are more subjective and stress subtle nuances and atmosphere. Although there is considerable diversity in size, type of instruments, style, and function among the various Balinese and Javanese gamelans, they all have a unique quality and basic characteristic which has long identified them with these islands. They represent the highest expression of musical art in these areas regardless of their association, whether it be with the wayangs, traditional dances, temple festivals, cremations, or other rituals. The present gamelans, in all probability, closely adhere in important aspects to the ancient types.

To date Western influence has been negligible except perhaps in some of the large, commercial seaport cities. Jakarta, the capital of Indonesia, the biggest of the seaport cities, has been most subjected to Western influence not only because of its vast commercial activity but because it was formerly the Dutch capital city of Batavia. Nevertheless, even here gamelan music still predominates. Radio Indonesia at Jakarta has a fine Javanese gamelan along with a Sundanese gamelan. Mr. Sudharnoto, Director of Radio Indonesia, indicated that about 10 per cent of the broadcast time is now given to Western music. He also explained that modern Sundanese melodies are very commonly programmed for radio as they have short phrases and rhythmically ordered meter (suggestive of Western) which is more easily assimilated by the divergent masses of people over the wide area that Radio Indonesia reaches. The increasing contact of these people with Western music, thought, philosophy, and procedures provokes some speculation as to the effect that Western civilization will ultimately have on their music.

CHAPTER II

Some Pertinent Attitudes

Western thought, developing along predominantly scientific lines, tends to categorize and attempts to standardize whatever it deals with, even the arts. Often this is not in accordance with some of the basic Oriental attitudes, and sometimes it produces misunderstandings and misconceptions not only in the arts but in all forms of intercourse as well. From the Book of Changes [1] one gleans that each event should be interpreted in its own context, that sensitivity to an object, event, or situation is basic. Absolute values, right or wrong, are at times questionable. Orientals have explained that cycles regulate life and that any positive rule of determinate meanings cannot be true at all times, because all determinate things are transitory.

Most Eastern religions do not recognize a determinate God as do Western religions. This produces a divergence of interpretation of determinate principles. In the East, the finite and the infinite are in different relationship with each other than in Western beliefs. Wisdom is fundamental and offers the vehicle for judgments; intelligence and determinate laws are secondary to it. Rabindranath Tagore in his essay on "What Is Art?" says:

> The West may believe in the soul of Man, but she does not really believe that the universe has a soul. Yet this is the belief of the East, and the whole mental contribution of the East to mankind is filled with this idea. So we, in the East, need not go into details and emphasize them; for the most important thing is this universal soul, for which the Eastern sages have sat in meditation, and Eastern artists have joined them in artistic realization. [2]

Oral tradition has been a prime method in the dissemination of knowledge in the Orient, and it still is in varying degrees in many areas. It is associated not only with primitive and ingenuous cultures but also with the highly

1. Book of Changes: a book of sixty-four essays of Chinese thought dealing with the ceaseless cycle of destruction and recreation in the world. It includes conceptions of Yin and Yang, Five Forces diagrams, etc. Possibly from early Chou times (1122–256 B.C.). Han writers considered it as a Confucian classic, but some of the material makes this doubtful.

2. From *Personality* by Rabindranath Tagore (New York: MacMillan Company, 1917), p. 36.

developed ones. In Java and Bali this oral tradition is still strongly maintained. However there are progressive teachers in the conservatories and universities who are considering the importance of written treatises and explanations of their music along with oral transmission. This trend will be valuable for enabling the Westerner to get a correct interpretation of true Javanese and Balinese viewpoints. But one must be cognizant that there is a considerable gap between oral tradition and written exposition in forwarding musical ideas. The latter, now evolving in Java and Bali, must still be interpreted with the latitude and lack of rigidity of the oral tradition rather than with the Western attitude of classification and rules (which must not be confused with principles).

At present in the study of this music many pitfalls confront those who are accustomed to relying on written, documented source material and notation. In regard to notation, many Oriental scholars have expressed to me the fear of artistic rigidity that is apt to result from standardized notation. In speaking to an Oriental scholar, Romain Rolland commented:

> Writing down our [Western] music has been not a little responsible for the fact that our art ages sooner than yours—as I was telling you. For while, on the one hand, a piece of music has the advantage of being stabilized and perpetuated the moment it is caught in the toils of a system of notation, on the other the advantage only accrues at the expense of its soaring capacity, a capacity that is generally retained intact by a music that is not standardized through being written down.[3]

At the Konservatori Karawitan Indonesia, Djurusan, Bali, a notation was being experimented with in which the tones were given a number such as 1, 2, 3, 4, 5 for slendro and 1, 2, 3, 4, 5, 6, 7 for pelog. This was not to regulate or to restrict pitches, but only to facilitate the learning of the cantus by the gamelan players. Books with cantus in Western notation were available at the Konservatori and at a few other places, but it must be realized that notes indicated in such books are only relative and not representative of a definite pitch of so many vibrations per second. For example, using a five-line staff, the five tones of slendro could be placed in a relative position such as:

3. Romain Rolland's conversation with philosopher Dilip Kumar Roy, from Dilip Kumar Roy, *Among the Great* (Bombay: Jaico Publishing House, 1950), pp. 39–40.

In this example, the Westerner thinks of exact-sized whole steps between 1 and 2, 2 and 3, and 4 and 5, and an exact-sized minor third between 3 and 4. As will be shown later, each gamelan is distinctive in the choice of pitches for the scale-tones. Thus the different intervals between the different numbers will vary from set to set, so that when playing the above example, the large interval could be between 1 and 2, or wherever the maker decided to put it. At the main music centers of Java, as in Jogjakarta and Surakarta, other notations of a more involved nature were being used, but these too were not standardized between places.

In the West, and in India and China, music practice developed, in all probability, simultaneously with theory. In contrast, the theory and historical development of Javanese and Balinese music is clouded. Their oral tradition gives more insight into practices and procedures than into origin or theories. In India the complex theory of Hindu music was outlined in chapters 28 through 33 of Bharata's *Natya Sastra* (c. 200 B.C.). In China, according to Laurence Picken:

> It was under the Hann Emperor Wuudih (141–87 B.C.) that the Imperial Bureau of Music (*Yuchfu*) was founded. This was responsible for supervising rites, ceremonies, and music of all kinds (foreign, court and folk music); for preparing archives of national melodies; and for establishing and maintaining the correct pitch of the *liulen*.[4,5]

An important difference in the application of these theories from those of Western music is the attitude toward them which permits great freedom through improvisation. Yet they are held within the scope of certain basic principles.

Some Western musicologists in attempting to establish and interpret theories of Javanese and Balinese music have given much valuable information. However, in their desire to categorize and to arrive at theoretical norms, some theories and terminologies have been advanced which are not acceptable to present-day Javanese and Balinese musical scholars. A *standardized* fixed pitch is alien to these scholars' conceptions. The idea of the rise or fall of an interval without exact or constant distance, as in the Chinese neumes, is more compatible. Even though the pitches of the gongs or of the individual bars or key-plates on any idiophone are approximately fixed because of the nature of their construction, an exact frequency for each tone is not considered paramount. Even on instruments of the same gamelan are found different frequencies for tones that are supposed to be the same pitch.

4. Laurence Picken, *The Music of Far Eastern Asia* from *Ancient and Oriental Music*, ed. Egon Wellesz (London: Oxford University Press, 1957), p. 96.

5. *Liulen* (liis, leu, luih): the twelve tones of the Chinese scale derived by cyclic fifths.

Often they merely simulate each other. Instruments of one gamelan, because of their pitches, frequently are not usable with those of a gamelan in another, even in an adjacent village, particularly if they have been made by different makers.

It was a fascinating and revealing experience to visit the different gamelan makers to watch them produce the instruments. Each artisan did his work in his home compound. Some craftsmen fashioned and carved the beautiful frames; others molded the bars for the idiophones; another matched bamboo resonators, while a man with a good ear advised on the tuning. Clay molds of approximate size were fashioned for the bars, kettles, and key-plates. A mixture of metals, the formula of which varied between makers, was poured into the molds before being heated. In the final stages, the bars were filed, the kettles or gongs were hammered to satisfactory pitches which were governed by the ear of the tuner or maker. Since the nem, or starting tone, was usually the highest tone that he could sing without effort, this resulted in a considerable range of tonality between gamelans. These variants gave each gamelan an individual quality.

The Indonesian government established a gamelan factory, Perusabaan Gamelan Negara Mangbunegara, in Surakarta, Java, in August, 1961, in order to standardize the intonation of gamelans. However, imitation still remains a basic factor. The principles and procedures of making the instruments are the same as before—where one man is the tuner and the several craftsmen working on the different gongs, bars, or kettles try to establish a pitch which has the approval of the tuner's ear—except that a set of tuned bars, evidently of Western make, was used as the pattern in the tuning for the establishment of a standardized norm for all gamelans made there. The scale-tones of this set were said to be duplicates of the scales of what they considered to be the best old gamelan, namely, that in the kraton of the susnan. Permission was given to record the tones of this set and they proved to have a fine, characteristic quality. The set had a Deagon identification plate on it, but the Deagon Company of Chicago later wrote that they had no record of having made this unusual set. The scales of these tuning bars will be analyzed in a later chapter along with scales from other typical and important gamelans.

One wonders if this attempt at standardization, with its resultant elimination of the appealing diversity and simple personality of each gamelan, might not be the first step toward its degeneration. In the main, it appeared that only those musicians in the few cities that have come under some Western influence are encouraging this standardization. To the average musician, particularly in the villages (where traditions are the strongest) it seemed incongruous.

Some Pertinent Attitudes

Throughout Indonesia one is aware of a politically inspired conception of the importance of a "National Image" (*Serampang duobelas*). The perpetrators of this notion seem to believe that uniformity is a needed feature and that it must be encouraged in every facet of national life to create unity from the many diverse, heterogeneous peoples of these islands with their different customs and languages. Whether this idea will ultimately dominate the arts is conjectural. What a fine and unique cultural National Image the traditional gamelans have been and should continue to be!

CHAPTER III

General Conceptions of Important Theoretical Tonal Systems

The musical sounds of the gamelans of Java and Bali will be more easily understood and appreciated if compared to established tonal systems and theories of other parts of the Orient and of the West. There are numerous ways in which a scale can be formed from a given tone. The most common ones in Western usage are Just intonation, or proportional ratios; the Pythagorean, or powers built on empirical fifths; and the Tempered system.

The Tempered system, in present use, is one in which the octave is arbitrarily divided into twelve equal parts. This produces a series of intervals which do not conform to the "natural" (pure) sounds of nature, as do the intervals arrived at by powers, ratios, multiple series of harmonics, natural division of string or tube length, etc. The Tempered system, which evolved with the development of harmony in the sixteenth and seventeenth centuries,[1] permits both vertical and linear construction and modulation between all keys. The intervals are simple and can be comprehended with a minimum of association by the large mass of people. The seeming complexity of the higher musical forms built on Tempered intonation results not from the actual, simple intervals themselves but from their combination and progression. The basic interval is the half step of 100 cents. All other intervals are a plural combination of this interval, such as the whole step of 200 cents, which is easily recognizable as consisting of two half steps, or a minor third as being a combination of three half steps.

Just and Pythagorean intonations were the basis for Western music prior to the advent of harmony and the Tempered system. They still influence it in hidden ways. All brass and woodwind instruments which produce several registers (or octaves) on one set of fundamentals pose factors of Just intonation which must be compensated for in the overall intonation plan. The tones used are "Just" overtones of the fundamentals of the instrument. The strings of the orchestra, which are tuned in perfect fifths, carry over some facets of Pythagorean intonation into the generally Tempered sound. The

1. 1533, first rules, LaFrance; 1588, in detail, Zarlino.

18

feeling for tonality is also very strong and induces players in the orchestra to alter tones from Tempered intonation to fit the particular key that is being used. Walter Piston in his essay "Intonation and Musical Meaning" states:

> If he [a student] has a good teacher he will have been made to notice that the third degree of a major scale is played sharp, very close to the fourth, and the seventh close to the tonic; and that the sixth degree of a minor scale is played low, close to the fifth, and so on. Playing in tune is more than a matter of the correct fingering on a stringed instrument, the right pattern of open and closed tone holes on the woodwind, or the proper valve combination on brass. Brass players, especially, know that virtually all tones have to be tempered by the lips to sound in tune.
>
> It should be emphasized that what is sought is not the sound of equal temperament. One seeks rather an intonation nearer to that of pure intervals and perhaps even more an underlining of musical meaning, which is closely tied traditionally to tonal feeling, the sense of key. The process is not scientific, but is one of tradition, handed down in the same way that musical meaning itself has grown. With most players this flexibility of pitch is introduced through habit, and more or less unconsciously, in the act of interpreting the printed notes in sound.[2]

The differences between the systems, however, are not too great, and the end product is acceptable in a system which relies mainly on harmonic sounds.

Just intonation is built on ratios. Using 1 as a starting point (for example, 100 vibrations per second [v.p.s.]), the octave will have the ratio of 2/1 or 200 v.p.s. The interval of the fifth will have the ratio of 3/2 or 150 v.p.s. Just intonation is characterized by whole steps of two different sizes: the major whole tone with a ratio of 9/8 and a value of 204 cents, and the minor whole tone with a ratio of 10/9 and a value of 182 cents. The difference between the two intervals is a syntonic comma of 22 cents. This comma is also found between a Just major third of 386 cents and a Pythagorean major third of 408 cents. In Hindu music, this interval of 22 cents is called the comma diesus (*diesus* means division), and is the common pramana, smallest of the regularly used intervals in Hindu music. It occurs between each pair of tones in the cycle of fourths and fifths in the series of twenty-two Hindu srutis (see Chart IV, pages 24–25). Commas occur in many places in the Just and Pythagorean systems. Ancient theorists worked with the idea of the natural division of the octave into fifty-two commas. This corresponded

2. From *Forum Series* (C. Bruno & Sons, Inc., 1963).

to the fifty-two distinct sounds of the old Sanskrit alphabet. These micro-tonal intervals with their capacity for subtle nuances, which are so characteristic of the highly developed melodic systems in some parts of the Orient, are not utilized in present Western music.

CHART II

INTERVALS WITHIN THE OCTAVE OF JUST INTONATION

Tone of Scale	Ratio to Preceding Tone	Cent Value from Preceding Tone	Cent Value from Tone Initial
1	1/1		
2	9/8	204	204
3	10/9	182	386
4	16/15	112	498
5	9/8	204	702
6	10/9	182	884
7	9/8	204	1088
8	16/15	112	1200

On this chart and all succeeding charts the cent values are given in whole numbers. In the event fractions occur, they have been omitted and the closest whole number substituted. For example, 204 is used as the value of a major whole tone, 9/8. In reality, it is 203.910.

Chart II lists the ratios, cent values, and vibrations per second of the common intervals within the octave in Just intonation. Using the ratios and cent values of this chart, one sees that if this series is applied to C Major starting on C, there will be a major whole tone of 204 cents between C (1) and D (2), also one between F (4) and G (5), and between A (6) and B (7). A minor whole tone of 182 cents is found between G (5) and A (6). Beginning the scale on G (with G as [1] in G Major), and using the Chart II series of ratios, the interval between G and A becomes a major whole tone of 204 cents and the one between A and B becomes a minor whole tone of 182 cents. Thus it can be seen that some tones in the G scale having the same pitch names as those in the C scale have different-sized whole tones. This variation in size of whole steps would also be found when comparing with other scales starting on other tones.

Pythagorean intervals are found by building upward by empirical fifths from any starting tone. For example, if one were to start with C, the first perfect fifth above C would be G, with a ratio of 3/2 and a value of 702 cents. When a fifth is added to this tone, $3/2 \times 3/2$, the resultant tone will be D with a cyclic ratio of 9/4, changed to 9/8 to correct the octave,[3] and with a cent value of 204 ($702 + 702 = 1404 - 1200$ (to correct octave) $= 204$). When a fifth is added above this D tone, the new tone is A with a ratio of 27/16, ($9/8 \times 3/2 = 27/16$), and with a cent value of 906 ($204 + 702 = 906$). Chart III below carries out the process of empirical fifths until the twelve tones of the octave are completed.

CHART III

Pythagorean Intervals

Arbitrarily starting on C!

	Number of Tone in Cycle of Fifths	Cent Value from Preceding Tone	Cent Value from Initial Tone
C	1	0	0
C♯	8	114	114
D	3	90	204
D♯	10	90	294
E	5	114	408
E♯ (F)	12	90	498
F♯	7	114	612
G	2	90	702
G♯	9	114	816
A	4	90	906
A♯	11	90	996
B	6	114	1110
B♯ (C)	13	90	1200

Intonation of the Renaissance period did not use cycle numbers 9, 10, and 11, but instead used only eight ascending fifths and three descending fifths. With C as the arbitrary starting tone, F of 498 cents, B♭ of 996 cents and E♭ of 294 cents were derived by the descending cycle of fifths.

In analyzing Chart III, several new intervals are found. The whole steps are all the same size, 204 cents, but the half steps are of two sizes: the hemitone of 90 cents and the large semitone of 114 cents. The difference

---

3. The denominator may be doubled to lower any ratio one octave.

between these two half steps is 24 cents, or a Pythagorean comma. This comma is also found when one compares the tone seven octaves above any starting tone to the *enharmonic* tone which results from building up twelve fifths from the starting tone. $(3/2)^{12} \times (2/1)^7 =$ a ratio of $\frac{531441}{524288}$. For example, using C_1 as the starting tone, C_8 will be seven octaves above. Using C_1 as the starting tone for a succession of twelve fifths, one arrives at B sharp$_7$, which is enharmonically the same as C_8 but which is 24 cents (a Pythagorean comma) sharper than C_8. The two half steps (hemitone and large semitone), and the one whole step combine to form intervals which vary from those of Just or Tempered intonation.

The three systems of Tempered, Just, and Pythagorean are compared to important Eastern theoretical systems (to be discussed shortly) in Chart IV, pages 24–25. In examination of this chart, one will notice that none of the arbitrary Tempered intervals are the same size as the natural (pure) intervals of any of the other theoretical systems. There is a difference in the sound of arbitrary intervals such as found in the Tempered system and the quality of tones in a system which can utilize the acoustical properties of sympathetic resonance which are present in the "natural" interval systems. Since quality of any musical tone is determined by the presence, strength, and arrangement of overtones to any fundamental, the systems employing natural intervals have an advantage along this line. While extensive harmony and modulation is not possible under the melodic systems using natural intervals, a harmonic quality or illusion is present, as it is in all modal systems. The constant sounding of a drone is typical in modal music. The Greeks called it mesa; the Byzantine called it ison; the Hindus call it shadja. A drone generates a very faint, subtle overtone series above it, and its persistence gives a harmonic illusion.

Certain theoretical systems of the Orient utilize some of the principles of Just and Cyclic intonations. They are highly refined and include microtonic intervals carried to the smallest degree believed possible for the trained human ear to assimilate. As a result, microtones of many sizes are used in contrast to the few restricted large intervals of Western music. A Western ear familiar with Tempered intervals has difficulty at first in recognizing and distinguishing the small intervals. Once they are heard and their relationship comprehended, new tonal vistas open.

The Hindu Raga and Chinese Ch'in systems represent the highest achievement in microtonal melodic music. Because of the subtle tonal shading of intervals, combination of pitched instruments is restricted, resulting in a very intimate sound of relatively low dynamic level.

The Hindu system, based on principles established in approximately the second century before the Christian era, commonly uses twenty-two srutis, a sruti being a definitely defined microtonal subdivision of the octave. They are arrived at by building up a cycle of fifths and a cycle of fourths from any reference tone or fundamental. This fundamental is not a fixed pitch with a definite number of vibrations per second, but can be of any frequency and is called Shadja or Sa. All ratios used in computing the intervals are arrived at from the chord of nature, which is the fundamental of any pitch and its overtone series. The fundamental of the chord of nature is considered to be 1. The ratio from the fundamental to the second partial or first overtone, which is an octave above the fundamental, is 2/1. The second overtone or third partial, which is a twelfth above the fundamental, has the ratio 3/1. The third overtone or fourth partial, which is a double octave above the fundamental, has the ratio of 4/1; etc. A tone can be reduced an octave by doubling the denominator. Example: if the denominator of the octave (2/1) is doubled (2/2), the tone is lowered one octave and is the same as the fundamental. If in the ratio 3/1 the denominator is doubled (3/2), the interval of a twelfth is reduced one octave and becomes a fifth above the fundamental; it is then a tone within the same octave as the fundamental.

Starting with any fundamental (Sa) as 1, one may multiply this by 3/2, which is the ratio of a perfect fifth. This produces Pa or sruti no. 14, column V in Chart IV. This is the second tone in the cycle of fifths. This ratio (3/2) is then multiplied by another fifth (3/2), which equals 9/4 (3/2 × 3/2 = 9/4). This when reduced within the ambit of an octave becomes 9/8, the third tone in the cycle of fifths and no. 5 in column V of Chart IV. The ratio 9/8 multiplied by another perfect fifth (3/2) equals 27/16 (9/8 × 3/2 = 27/16). This is sruti no. 18 of column V and the fourth tone in the cycle of fifths. 27/16 × 3/2, the next perfect fifth, equals 81/32, or 81/64 when the register is corrected. This is no. 9 in column V. This procedure is continued through eleven fifths.

The same process is used in arriving at the tones derived from the cycle of perfect fourths. The ratio 1/1 is again considered the first tone of the cycle, the same initial tone as used in the cycle of fifths. Starting with the fundamental as 1, one may multiply this by 4/3, which is the ratio of the perfect fourth. This produces Ma, the second tone in the cycle of fourths, listed as sruti no. 10 in column V. The ratio 4/3 multiplied by another perfect fourth (4/3) equals 16/9, or sruti no. 19 in column V. This is the third tone in the cycle of fourths. 16/9 × 4/3 equals 32/27, the fourth tone in the cycle of fourths, or sruti no. 6 in column V. This is continued through eleven ascending fourths, the same as was done in the cycle of fifths.

Combining the eleven tones of the cycle of fourths with the eleven tones of the cycle of fifths results in twenty-two sruti tones within the Indian

CHART IV

COMPARATIVE CHART OF TONES WITHIN THE OCTAVE OF IMPORTANT THEORETICAL MUSICAL SYSTEMS

I Number of Cents Above Fundamental	II Tempered		III Just (Using C as Tonic)[4]			IV Pythagorean			V Hindu			VI Blown fifths — Basis for Chinese Liu	VII String Length Division — Principle for traditional Chinese and Japanese String Instruments.[10]	
	Name	Interval	Ratio	Interval	Name	Cycle No.	Interval	Name	Ratio	Sruti No.	Name[7]	Appearance in Cycle	Vibrating Length	Interval
0	C	Unison	1/1	Unison	C	0	Unison	C	1/1		Sa	1		
22									81/80	1 Pramana				
24						12	Comma					17		
48														
90							Minor 2nd (Limma[5])	Db	256/243	2	Ri			
100	Db	Half step												
102														
112									16/15	3	Ri			
114						7	Aug. Prime	C#				10		
156												3		
182									10/9	4	Ri			
200	D	Whole step												
204			9/8	Whole step	D	2	Maj. 2nd	D	9/8	5	Ri			
231												19	7/8	Large Whole tone
258												12		
294							Min. 3rd (3rd of desc. cycle[6])	Eb	32/27	6	Ga			
300	Eb	Minor 3rd												
312												5		
316									6/5	7	Ga		5/6	Minor 3rd
318						9	Aug. 2nd	D#						
360												21		
386			5/4	Major 3rd	E				5/4	8	Ga		4/5	Major 3rd
400	E	Major 3rd												
408						4	Major 3rd	E	81/64	9	Ga			
414												14		
468												7		
498			4/3	Perfect 4th	F		Perfect 4th (1st in desc. cycle)	F	4/3	10	Ma		3/4	Perfect 4th
500	F	Perf. 4th												
516												23		
520									27/20	11	Ma			
570												16		

Cents	Equal-temp. note / interval	Ratio / interval	Cycle no. / interval	Note (1#)	Ratio	Sruti no.	Pa (sargam)	Blown no.	Ratio	Interval
612			6 — Aug. 4th		64/45	13				
624										
678										
700										
702	G Perf. 5th	3/2 Perf. 5th	1 — Perf. 5th	G	3/2	14		9 2	2/3	Perfect 5th
726										
780										
792					128/81	15	Fa	18 11		
800										
814	G# Aug. 5th		8 — Aug. 5th	G#	8/5	16	Dha			
816										
834										
882										
884	A Maj. 6th	5/3 Maj. 6th	3 — Maj. 6th	A	5/3	17	Dha	4 20	3/5	Major 6th
900										
906					27/16	18	Dha			
936										
990										
996	A# Aug. 6th		Min. 7th (2nd of desc. cycle)	Bb	16/9	19	Dha	13 6		
1000										
1018			10 — Aug. 6th	A#	9/5	20	Ni			
1020										
1038								22		
1088	B Maj. 7th	15/8 Maj. 7th	5 — Maj. 7th	B	15/8	21	Ni			
1092							Ni	15		
1100										
1110					243/128	22	Ni			
1146										
1200	C Perf. 8ve	2/1 Perf. 8ve		C				8	1/2	Octave
1586									2/5	Octave + Maj. 3rd
1902									1/3	Octave + Perf. 5th
2400									1/4	2nd Octave
3172									1/5	2nd Octave + Maj. 3rd
3804									1/6	2nd Octave + Perf. 5th
4800									1/8	3rd Octave

4. Just ratios may start with any tonic or reference tone. Actual pitch will vary according to tonic tone chosen, but ratios and cent values will remain constant above any tonic.

5. Limma: common interval of difference between the regular scale steps. Another interval of difference is one of 114 cents. See page 21, column 3 of Chart III, and page 26.

6. Descending cycle: see page 37.

7. For complete name, derivation from cycle, type of sruti, etc., see *Tones and Intervals of Hindu Music* by Donald A. Lentz (Lincoln: University of Nebraska Press, 1961).

8. See pages 19–26.

9. Blown fifths: Von Hornbostel's fifth of an average cent value of 678 is used as a basis of comparison. See page 27.

10. See page 28.

octave, as shown in column V, Chart IV. Examination of the chart reveals many small intervals of varying sizes not found in Tempered intonation but all being natural intervals as found in Just or Pythagorean intonations. There are three common, simple intervals. It is interesting to note that the comma which is called the pramana sruti in the Hindu system occurs between each pair of the cycle of fourths and fifths. It has a ratio of 81/80 and a cent value of 22. It is the difference between a Just major tone and minor tone; $9/8 \div 10/9 = 81/80$. The nyuna is the most unusual of the intervals insofar as Western consideration is concerned. It is 70 cents in size with a ratio of 25/24 and is comparable to an interval called a minor semitone. It is the difference between a Just minor tone, 10/9, and a Just semitone. The third interval, the purana, is the old Greek limma, or hemitone of Pythagorean tuning. It has a cent value of 90 and a ratio of 256/243. These three sruti are combined to form larger sruti. A dvisruti, made up of a purana and a pramana, has a ratio of 16/15 and equals 112 cents or a Just major semitone. The trisruti, 10/9, is formed by three sruti, namely, a purana, a nyuna, and a pramana, totaling 182 cents, that of a Just minor tone. The chatussruti, or Just major whole tone (9/8 or 204 cents), is commonly a combination of a purana, nyuna, and two pramana sruti. A panchasruti (32/37, 294 cents) comprises five smaller sruti. A shatsruti (6/5, 316 cents) is made up of six smaller sruti.

The selection of srutis from the twenty-two available for the seven, six, or five tones (svaras) of the raga, their proper relationship in the two tetrachords,[11] the tones used as embellishments (gamalkas), the slighted tones (alpatvas) and the selection of principal, functional, and final tones (vadis, samvadis, grahas) create a most diverse, melodically expressive system. The absence of set pitches (definite frequencies) and the improvisatory nature of treatment make this a thoroughly Oriental and definitely great theoretical system. Its influence on the higher forms of music in a large area of Southeast Asia is pronounced. As stated before, Hindu culture dominated Java and Bali from about the first century A.D. to the thirteenth, and is still in strong evidence in present-day Bali. In spite of this, it will be noted in succeeding chapters how meager are the influences of this powerful music on the gamelan music. Yet it is necessary to know the basis of the two primary theoretical systems of the Orient, important from ancient times on, in order to evaluate the music of Java and Bali.

The second great theoretical system, developed in China, has influenced in varying degrees the music of Japan, Korea, Manchuria, Laos, Vietnam,

11. Tetrachord: originally four sounds within the range of a perfect fourth. Later conceived as a lower sphere of the four lowest tones of a scale and an upper sphere of the four highest tones.

and Tibet. The pentatonic facet of it may have been transmuted into the slendro mode of Javanese and Balinese music. Though the Chinese system is very different from the Hindu, it has been a melodic system which has used many small intervals which are likewise arrived at by means of Cyclic or Just (string-length division) procedures. The traditional Chinese classical music being considered must not be confused with the noisy clash and din of present-day popular Chinese opera. The dominant features of the classical forms are the combination of set and indeterminate pitches and the total lack of rigidity. Chinese speech is monosyllabic and with each word the meaning can change according to inflection of the voice. The word can remain level, it can rise, or it can fall; it can also vary according to the stress. Chinese music, thought to have derived originally from language, follows the idea of the neumes. These provide the direction of inflection of a word, but *not* the *exact* distance. Stress is determined by melodic movement. In Western speech the contour of word groupings is apt to depend upon the emotional interpretation of the words. In Chinese speech, the type of neumes outlines an intellectualized flow. Phonology is to Chinese music as calligraphy is to Chinese painting.

Two theoretical systems evolved in China, one derived from the Cyclic Pentatonic and the other from the division of string lengths. They are found combined in the highest form of Ch'in music. The Cyclic Pentatonic, arrived at mathematically, is important in Chinese musical thought. The conception of the twelve liis (tones) dates back to the Han dynasty.[12] They are formed by building empirical fifths in a manner similar to that used in Pythagorean tuning. Methods of arriving at these fifths included the use of twelve tubes. Levis[13] indicates that a stopped bamboo tube 230 millimeters long, 8.12 millimeters in diameter, and vibrating at 366 vibrations per second was the Yellow Bell (Huang Chong), the standard established by the Bureau of Weights and Measures in 239 B.C. Tube number two was made two-thirds the length of the reference tube; number three was made equal to two-thirds of number two and then doubled to bring the tone within the ambit of an octave. This process was repeated for each of the twelve tubes. The fifths produced by these tubes were small compared to Western fifths. Various musicologists place them between 670 to 680 cents as compared to the Just fifth of 702 cents. Dr. E. M. von Hornbostel, after studying blown tubes and considering all factors, including end correction, advanced an hypothesis in his *Anthropos* (1919) that Blown fifths which are derived as

12. Han dynasty: ruled China from 206 B.C. to A.D. 220. An era of expansion and cultural growth.

13. John Hazedel Levis, *Foundations of Chinese Musical Art* (Peiping: Henri Vetch, 1936), p. 27.

overtones from a stopped bamboo tube of the dimension of the Yellow Bell have an average cent value of 678. As an addendum, it is interesting to note that von Hornbostel's Blown fifth interval requires a cycle of twenty-three fifths to arrive at the enharmonic tone equivalent to the reference tone. It differed from the reference tone, after being brought within the ambit of an octave, by a comma of only six cents:

$$1200 \times 13 = 15600 \text{ cents (Octaves)}$$
$$678 \times 23 = \underline{15594} \text{ cents (Blown fifths)}$$
$$6 \text{ cents (Comma difference)}$$

In Java musicians and gamelan makers, when queried about the small fifth, explained it as coming from nature but gave no specific examples. At dawn one morning in a small village in Java, a bird was singing with a call of an octave and a small fifth. This I recorded. The same song was frequently heard later and again recorded for confirmation of interval. It is a fascinating bit of fancy that the fifth in the bird call when measured on the stroboscope varied only two or three cents from the one of 678 cents. There are also indications that the small fifth might have been a standard in Sumeria and Egypt.

Examination of column VI of Chart IV illustrates the relationship of the tones derived from the Chinese Cyclic Fifth series with those of other systems. The early Chinese used the fundamental and first eleven Blown fifths to produce the twelve liis. From the twelve liis, five tones of consecutive Blown fifth order were chosen for a Cyclic Pentatonic scale. For example, C, G, D, A, and E produced the following pentatonic scale: C, D, E, G, A with no half steps or major thirds. This principle still exists in China. In the Hindu Raga system, any of the twenty-two srutis are available for choice of tones for a raga if they have the prescribed consonant relationship to the Sa (fundamental) and other tones. In the Chinese system this is not the case, for the tones have to be arrived at consecutively through the cycle of fifths. Transposition is possible by starting on a different lii.

In music for the ch'in, a zither-type instrument, the seven strings are tuned to the Cyclic Pentatonic. Each string has frets or nodes dividing it into the following lengths: 1/2, 1/3, 2/3, 1/4, 3/4, 1/5, 4/5, 1/6, 5/6, 1/8, and 7/8. The resultant cent values are listed in column VIII of Chart IV. Each string employs the principle of Just intonation, but many microtonic intervals result when this theory of string length division is combined with the above Cyclic Pentatonic procedure, which is used to tune the seven open strings. There is no counterpart in Western Tempered music. Many Oriental stringed instruments use frets which are movable. The accuracy of placing the fret, which is done by ear, can greatly affect the pitch and thus produce noticeable deviances in a system using natural intervals of micro-tonic size. The tones of the present-day scales of Japanese koto and gekkin music evolved with variance from the Ch'in principle.

Western musicians think of the fifth as being an interval of 700 to 702 cents. The deviation of only two cents between Just, Pythagorean, and Tempered fifths is so small that these sizes are accepted as being the true fifth. This is not the case in Oriental music, even though some Western musicologists try to explain their fifths as anomalies from the Western norm. The conception of the fifths is in many cases very different. For the most part they are smaller than the Western fifth. In Chinese music, another common theoretical fifth of 693 cents, as contrasted with the Cyclic fifth of 678 cents, results from combining three of the characteristic large seconds derived from string-length division (see column VII in Chart IV). Each of the large seconds has a value of 231 cents and a ratio of 8/7. In Hindu music, the seven svaras (tones) that the octave can be divided into are formed by different-sized srutis; the interval of the fifth, five svaras above the starting tone, can vary in size from nine to thirteen srutis.

Fifths of varying sizes are produced on different pipes when the end-correction factor is not considered, thus not fitting a theoretical system. These convert to a standard when duplicated. This procedure of duplication is found in China along with the theoretical fifth, and although one cannot find positive documentation of it for the gamelans of Java and Bali, it is highly possible that it became a factor in the varying sizes of the fifth there too.

Some Indonesian musicians considered a tone produced five keys from a reference key or five finger holes above a specific hole on a flute as a fifth. The significant factor is that the fifths of Oriental systems vary and may not conform to Western standards. This is also true of all intervals except the primes and octaves.

CHAPTER IV

A Commentary on Oriental Primitive Music

Some cursory comments on the primitive music of Southeast Asia is also in order before proceeding to the considerations of Javanese and Balinese gamelans. There are groups of peoples in areas of Southeast Asia who fall into the classification of primitive. Their customs, art, and music are definitely on this level. The most elemental types of instruments and forms of melodic tonal arrangements are found among them. An example of a rudimentary type instrument is the jaw's harp, made from a leaf of a langkop palm, which produces only two tones. It is common among the Semelais in Malaya and is also found in remote areas in Sumatra and in other Indonesian regions. The quaint tonal sound has a pleasing effect. The tones vary from instrument to instrument as each is made by the individual player. One jaw's harp that I recorded produced an F twenty-five cents flat from the Tempered F and E flat thirty-five cents flat. In contrast, another jaw's harp produced a C sharp which was eighteen cents sharp and an A thirty-two cents sharp.

Elemental melodies resulting from constant repetitions of a motive often made up of just a tone with upper and lower neighboring tones are encountered. Rhythmic variants of such a motive seem to indicate a higher step of attainment. The interval of a fifth is a further expansion and is found more often than the minor third in the simple music. In general the vocal range as well as the number of tones used is restricted. In the Temiar group in Malaya, up to four tones were used in one of the numbers. The tones were roughly as follows: F sharp about 38 cents sharp from Tempered, G sharp about 50 cents flat, A sharp about 45 to 50 cents flat, and C sharp about 25 cents flat. Although the music usually is but a single-line melody, more advanced types do at times have a responsorial effect created when a motive is sung by a solo voice and answered verbatim or with slight modification by a chorus. Repetitious rhythmic patterns of short length are usually metered. When they are unmetered they tend to follow vocal syllabic accents and quantities. The latter should not be confused with or thought to be derived from the highly organized, unmetered rhythmic patterns of the

Hindu Tala[1] system. Even in India primitive groups are found whose music is limited and elementary, as among the Santhals and the Assamese.

It is difficult to classify primitive music and to measure its intervals. With vocal pitches it is virtually impossible, for they are frequently unstable. In some instances the musical tones have evolved from the sound language (similar to the Chinese neumes); in others the restrictions of size, shape, or placement of holes or frets on an instrument are a determining factor. In general the tonal ranges are limited, frequently not greater than a fourth or fifth. The flattened fifth and wide second seem quite common. The major third is definitely a product of a more highly developed system.

Bamboo flutes are common among such peoples. While no two are apt to have the same pitches due to the cutting of the holes to fit the fingers of each player, the pitches of each flute are fairly stable. The following tones, found on a three-toned nose flute from Semai-Senoi, Ulu Slin in South Perak, is typical: F, thirteen cents sharp; A, correct with Tempered A 440; and B, five cents flat. A flute accompanying some dances in Negri Sembilan had the following approximate tones: C sharp, seven cents sharp; F sharp, six cents sharp; G sharp, 20 cents flat; A sharp, thirty-one cents flat; and B, eighteen cents flat. F sharp was the important tone in the melody. These are typical examples.

In between the simple music with two to four tones and the highly complex theoretical systems are many intermediate types. These can be elaborations of the primitive forms, or degenerations of the complex theories, or more or less independently conceived systems which may have developed and persisted for centuries through duplication. Some of the intermediate types possess a vital, individual, indigenous character, but their true derivation and background are not always distinctly apparent.

It is revealing to note the reaction of Westerners when hearing tapes or records of primitive music and those of highly developed Hindu Raga or Chinese Ch'in or Japanese Koto or Gagaku music for the first time. Because of lack of familiarity with the intervals, quality of sound, rhythms, and structures, the tendency at first is to place the primitives and the theoretical forms in the same category when in reality, they may be poles apart. In order to understand and appreciate music of the Orient, it is necessary to gain an acquaintance not only with the technical phases but also with the actual sound of the music and with the temper of the particular cultures.

1. Tala: highly evolved Hindu Classic rhythmic system.

CHAPTER V

Ingenuous ?[1]

Few, if any, of the basic elements of the theories of the well-defined and documented Hindu Raga conception or of higher Chinese forms are in evidence in Balinese or Javanese gamelan music. It is true that the five-tone scale (slendro) has a suggested counterpart in the Chinese Cyclic Pentatonic, but the derivation, selection, and use of tones, interval size and relationship, and other factors, show no similarity between the two systems. This will be explained in more detail a little later. One might feel that the improvisatory treatment of certain aspects of Indonesian gamelan music might possibly be a result of Hindu influence, but the wide tonal exploitation with the subtle nuances and soaring flexibility of Raga improvisation has little in common with the metric treatment, elaboration, and embellishment that is part of the gamelan tradition. The latter follows a definite format and sequential order and has a restricted tonal selection. It is, however, much more advanced than the whimsical strophic style and quasi-heterophonic treatment found in the forms of the primitives.

Cosmic consciousness, because of the close integration with religion, seems to influence the *emotional* attitude toward music in India and Indonesia. Since the Moslems who arrived in Java and other parts of Indonesia in the thirteenth century came primarily from India, an attitude against music was not as prevalent among them as among some of the rigidly orthodox of the Middle East Islamic countries. Under the Moslems the emphasis changed from the temple and festival activity of the people to the needs of court ceremonies and entertainment except in Bali, where the prior Hindu culture, by then synthesized with the indigenous, remained uppermost. In general, outside theoretical musical influences in Indonesia seem to be minimal.

The indications are that the gamelans are ingenuous to Java and Bali. These have been grouped together in this study because their basic structures, kinds of instruments, color of sound (due to idiophones), concept of system,

1. Ingenuous: used in this book in the sense that its meaning does not include a planned, rationalized, or studied evolution, but rather something springing from response to elemental beauty and expression and maintaining its continuity from the same source.

formal structures, and rhythmic formats are generically similar. The minor differences really identify each with the differences in the two cultures. The positive, brilliant sound of the Balinese instruments ties in perfectly with the outgoing Balinese nature and with the communal, agrarian type of life in Bali. The people are the participants. In contrast, the refined, often esoteric, rarefied sound of the Javanese gamelan is easily associated with the elegance and former power of the courts of the sultanates. The people are the audience.

Few works have been written by Balinese or Javanese explaining the theoretical basis for the gamelans. Documented historical background for the art is almost nonexistent. It has been only recently that a few have resorted to written elucidation as a supplement to the established procedures of oral tradition. The musical scholars were most generous and thorough in offering explanations of the gamelan concepts, however, and from these discussions significant facts emerged. In general they place a different stress on and attach less significance to historical theoretical origins and development than is found in the sequential, empirical thinking of most Westerners.

The gamelan music of Java and Bali shows every evidence of having evolved in a manner other than that of the theoretical systems of the Hindu Raga and Chinese Cyclic. Whereas the two latter have their roots in ordered and planned acoustical phenomena, the gamelans show their development as being more of a casual growth linked strongly to the traditional and to the ceremonial and religious expressions. To gain an overall comprehension of this ingenuous system, important theoretical elements will next be considered.

Scale Derivation

Three basic tones and two or four secondary tones are the background of the gamelan tonal system. The main tone, called dong in Bali, is supported by two tones, one a fifth above (called dang) and the other a fifth below (called dung). The secondary tones are a fifth above (dèng) and a fifth below (ding) the supporting tones. By bringing the five tones within an octave, the following scale results: dong, dèng, dung, dang, ding.

An interesting observation is found in comparing the pentatonic scale developed from this treatment of fifths with that of the pentatonic produced by the Chinese Cyclic or Pythagorean systems. For convenience the tone names of Western notation will be used, with C arbitrarily chosen as a starting tone. But it should be recalled that the Oriental fifths are variable in size and in all probability will not correspond to a Western fifth.

Balinese-Javanese:

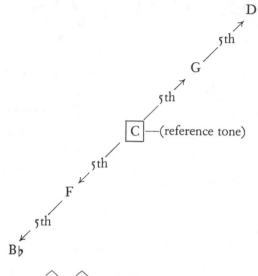

equals C D F G B♭ C when placed within an octave.

Chinese Cyclic Pentatonic:

equals C D E G A C when placed within an octave.

In the Balinese-Javanese five-tone scale, a large interval, approximately a minor third, which will vary in size from one gamelan to the next, occurs between the second and third and the fourth and fifth degrees. In the Chinese Cyclic Pentatonic, the large interval is between the third and fourth and the fifth and sixth (octave tone) degrees. This clarifies the difference in scale derivation referred to earlier in the chapter.

Ki Sindoesawarno, who also has a good knowledge of Hindu and Western music, wrote the following to me in a letter (in English) dated December 30, 1962:

Dong—dèng—dung—dang—ding are still the Balinese names of the gamelan-tones for both slendro and pelog. There are many evidences to be found assuring that those names were *the* original names in all areas of Indonesia. These are onomatopoetical, as appears from the dental ḍ, which points to some struck instrument, and the nasal -ng, which points to a bright, metallic tone. The vowels o—è—u —a—i represent the *succession* of the tones in the scale. This succession looks somewhat strange to us, but apparently contains the key of the tonal structure of the gamelan.

When we arrange the vowels in *gradation of quality*, the succession must be: o—u—a—è—i. This gradation of quality is descriptively explained in the following example. "Sr" is a stem word imitating a water-stream. Therefore, "*sor*" is a big and violently falling stream, "*sur*" a less violent one, "*sar*" a stream in any direction, "*sèr*" a moderate, horizontal stream and "*sir*" a fine, small stream. This way of describing a grade of quality is characteristic in our language. So, dong—dung—dang—dèng—ding are decreasing grades of quality, and strikingly so. This succession of decreasing qualities is at the same time a succession of functional subordination in musical melody. The suborder of functions in every paṭet looks like this:

dong—tonic—graha (Indian)—bakuswara (Javanese).
dung—subdominant ⎫
dang—dominant   ⎬—important tones—dajaswara (Jv.)
dèng—passing tone ⎫
ding—passing tone ⎬—supplying tones—wargaswara (Jv.)

In visually more understandable structure:

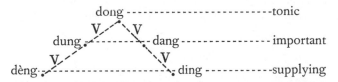

It needs no further comment that the sequence of qualities in the names represents the functional gradation of the tones in active melody. The individual name of each tone includes its own function in every melodic form.

The intervals from left upwards and then downwards, dèng— dung—dong—dang—ding, are apparently fifths, here marked by V. Once again, frappant! Those fifths arrange themselves in literary and musical order. Those fifths brought back into one octave form the succession of tones in the scale again: o—è—u—a—i, which does not look strange any more.

These facts cannot be a mere coincidence. It must be or must have been a well organized onomatopoeia in a phylological and musicological sense. And so it appears that the Indonesian Karawitan[2] has this characteristic in tone-notation. This notation was well-known in

2. Karawitan: music school.

all gamelan-areas in Indonesia. Many remainders of it are there, but at present is only practically used in the Balinese Karawitan. When we now shape a relation between the present Balinese and Javanese musical notes, the proper way is in their functional relation in the melody, i.e., in the paṭet-order, and not in intervals and absolute pitches.

This letter emphasizes not only the importance of functional relationships which are characteristic of the gamelan system, but also the fact that these tone-terms originally were possibly used in both Java and Bali. They are not commonly employed in Java today. Instead, designation by key-plates (which are fixed pitch) on the idiophone instruments is more common. The names of each of the key-plates (or metal bars) moving from left to right on the slendro instruments are: gulu, dada, lima, nem, barang. This method recognizes the names of the tones as the Western method recognizes the C, D, E, etc. keys on a piano. The *dong—dang—dung* method recognizes the *function* of the tone as the Western method recognizes the function of a tonic, dominant, and subdominant in any key. Throughout Bali the gamelan players, when questioned about the pitches, answered by calling the key-plates by the names of dong, dang, dung, etc. This indicates the limited function there of the key-plate tone and the restriction as to mode as compared to Javanese usage of key-plate names. In the latter system, the important tone dong can be shifted to different key-plates, thus producing different tonalities comparable to those of the Western modes.

Paṭet

Paṭet[3] is the Javanese term meaning "harmonious" and refers to the location of the principal tone and its related tones on the bars of an instrument. A Western interpretation of paṭet has been "classification," but it could be considered as being comparable to an early European mode. In Bali, because of the functional association of the dong, dang, dung, etc. with specific key-plates or bars, shifting of tonality is more restricted, so the Balinese word paṭut is not as commonly employed. However, in some areas gamelans of flutes were called suling paṭut, and in others angklung gamelans were called anklung paṭut. The term laras, which in a general sense means scale, is more commonly used instead of paṭut by the Balinese to classify mode.

Chart V illustrates how the dong—dang—dung conception was originally

3. Mantle Hood of the University of California at Los Angeles has given a detailed analysis and interpretation of paṭet in his book *The Nuclear Theme as a Determinant of Paṭet in Javanese Music* (Djakarta: J. B. Wolters-Groningen, 1954).

CHART V

PAṬET

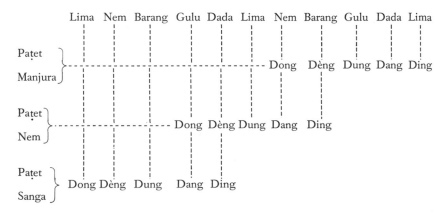

used with the Javanese key-names. Placing the dong on different key-plates changes the paṭet. It is important to realize that from any dong (basic tone) the dung is a fifth below and the dang a fifth above. This restricts the place where the dong can be located because of the limited number of fifths within a pentatonic along with the limited number of key-plates on instruments. This has resulted in three principal paṭets being recognized in the slendro (five-tone) scale. The size of the fifths are not as important as the fact that they must be complementary. When the dung is raised an octave, it forms a fourth above the dong or a second with the dang. The size of these two intervals can vary without unmusical effects if the original fifths are agreeable.

Along this line Ki Sindoesawarno states in his letter of December 30, 1962:

> As to the names of paṭets, the following reconstruction is given. Our instrumentalists valued tonic (= dong), subdominant (= dung) and dominant (= dang) as the most important tones. When such an important tone occasionally was the fifth key-plate (from left) on his gender, the player easily called the paṭet "the mode of the fifth plate"; that is to say: paṭet Lima. When it was the sixth, the paṭet was called paṭet Nem, and means "the mode of the sixth plate or tone." There were two periods in the gender evolution in which such name-giving occurred. The first period [ancient] was that of the gender-sepuluh, i.e., gender with 10 plates. The present gender-wayang in Bali and some old-fashioned Javanese gender types are the undestroyable representatives. On such a gender the first key-plate on the left hand

side was the present Javanese Gulu, corresponding with dong. From this we have:

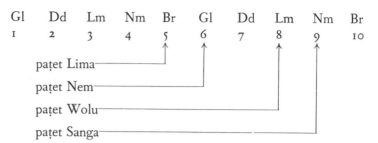

Gl	Dd	Lm	Nm	Br	Gl	Dd	Lm	Nm	Br
1	2	3	4	5	6	7	8	9	10

patet Lima
patet Nem
patet Wolu
patet Sanga

Gender	Serial No. of Plate	Function	Name of Patet
Pelog (Bem-type)	5	dong/dung	Lima (= 5)
Slendro and Pelog	6	dong	Nem (= 6)
Slendro and Pelog	8	dong	Wolu (= 8)
Slendro and Pelog	9	dong	Sanga (= 9)

In that period these names were popular in all gamelan-areas, and there were no other names.

In accordance with the development of elaboration in the instrumental gender-play and in the vocal melodic and rhythmic improvisation, the gender-10 meanwhile developed into the gender-sawelas (gender-11), in which a "small" Gulu was added at the right border. Later on the gender-11 obtained a lower Barang-plate at the left side, and thus the gender-12 came into existence. At last the gender-13 came into being when a higher Dada at the right side was added. This is the gender-telulas in Java as well as in Bali and elsewhere. Gender-14 with an added lower Nem at left side is among the luxurious types. What had happened in this second period to the name-giving? The left-hand patets Lima and Nem preserved their names without objection, for those were easy enough to be recognized. The right-hand patets Wolu and Sanga, on the contrary, caused confusing troubles on the "modern" gender-13. Supposing in a performance it is said: "Let us play in patet Sanga." What would be wanted in point of fact?

The "new" patet Sanga was the ancient patet Wolu, and the "old" patet Sanga was now the patet Sepuluh (= 10)! Therefore, a new terminology was put in circulation in accordance with gender-13. But the more conservative gamelan-areas, preserving the gender-10 habits, prefer the old names to the new ones, in spite of the fact that the gender-13 as an instrument gradually found acceptance in those areas too. Thus the somewhat confusing terminology in patet name-giving evolved, particularly in Eastern-Java in comparison with Mid-Java.

Yet every serious musician is still able to recognize those paṭet-names from each other and to use them correctly.

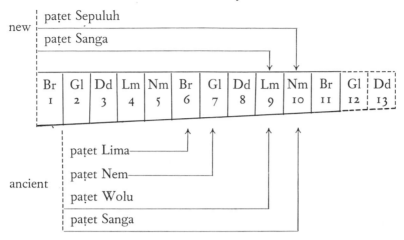

For the sake of clearness the following scheme of the paṭet-names, current nowadays, is presented. Mark (n) means new, derived from gender-13; unmarked, the contrary: derived from gender-10.

	Mid-Java	Eastern Java
Slendro:		
dong = Gl	paṭet Nem	paṭet Sepuluh (n)
dong = Lm	paṭet Sanga (n)	paṭet Wolu
dong = Nm	paṭet Manjura (n)	paṭet Sanga
Pelog:		
dong = Gl	paṭet Nem	paṭet Nem
dong = Lm	paṭet Lima	paṭet Wolu
dong = Nm	paṭet Barang (n)	paṭet Sanga

The paṭets are used practically. Every instrumentalist knows them, feels them and respects them. The vocalist feels them and has himself obediently bound to them. The average auditor is aware of or senses their existence but does not always know or feel them. The theorist understands them.

These comments and analyses by an Indonesian of Ki Sindoesawarno's stature clarify some of the problems of paṭet concept for the Westerner.

Slendro and Pelog

Two basic scale patterns are used in both Java and Bali: slendro and pelog. In general, the slendro has five tones of fairly similarly-sized intervals. Some of the anklung gamelans of Bali are exceptions and have only four tones.

CHART VI

IG. B. N. PANDJI'S EXPLANATION OF INTERVAL SIZES

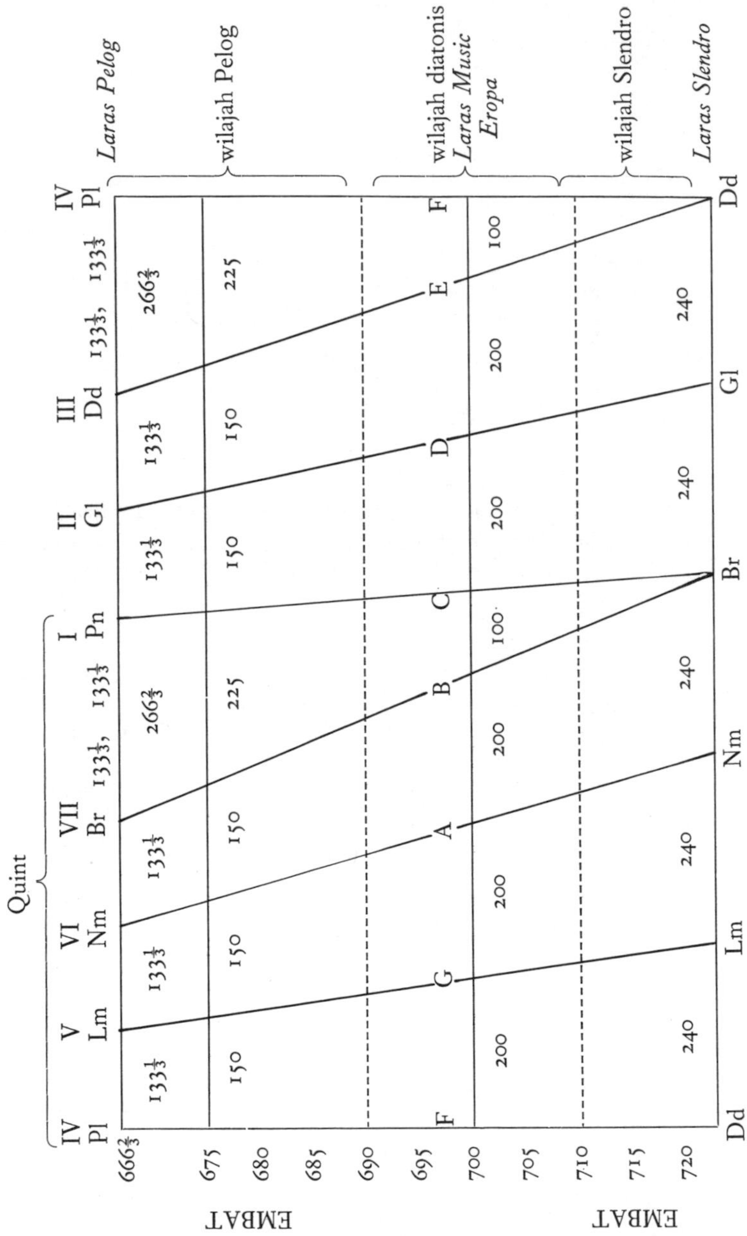

Embat: spread out, variable. *Wilajah*: area. *Laras*: in a general sense, scale.

The pelog may vary somewhat, but it is usually thought of as a seven-tone scale of varying large and small intervals. There are still five primary tones in pelog which correspond to dong, dèng, dung, dang, ding. The two remaining tones are considered as being auxiliary, inasmuch as they divide each of the two large intervals and are used secondarily to the primary tones. Singers may use the auxiliary tones as embellishments. The acceptance of indefinite interval size is important. The examples of intervals measured from tapes taken of gamelans, which appear in a later chapter, will confirm this impression.

IG. B. N. Pandji, an authoritative Balinese scholar, has graciously supplied the chart, designated as Chart VI, which illustrates his method of explaining to his students the intervals in slendro and pelog. It also shows the attitude toward the varying size of the fifth. In Chart VI the fifth in pelog is 675 cents (though it can vary from $666\frac{2}{3}$ to 690), while in slendro it turns out to be 720 cents. In actual practice few gamelans have intervals of 150 or 225 cents as in pelog; the same is true of the interval of 240 cents in slendro. These are only approximations of interval size. The intervals would lose some of their charm and ingenuous quality if they adhered to the exact subdivisions as illustrated on the chart. Again it must be stressed, as IG. B. N. Pandji explained in our discussions, that this chart is considered only as an *aid* to show *in general* the varying systems and is not meant to be rigidly adhered to, as a Westerner would interpret a chart of our Tempered or Just intonations.

The following is an excerpt from IG. B. N. Pandji's letter of January 9, 1963, in which he explains the material in Chart VI:

> Didalam Karawitan untuk memudahkan menghitung sruti2 itu, maka dipergunakan satuan jaitu: cent (bagian); djadi djarak 1 oktaf dibagi mendjadi 1200 cents.
>
> Laras Pelog, laras Musik Eropa dan laras Slendro mempunjai djarak2 jang sama, jaitu dalam 1 oktaf = 1200 cents.
>
> Pada kwint 675 cents ternjata laras itu adalah laras Pelog sama rata; jaitu sruti2 jang ketjil semuanja 150 cents dan sruti2 jang besar 225 cents.
>
> Pada kwint 700 cents ternjata laras itu adalah laras Musik Eropa (Diatonis).
>
> Pada kwint 720 cents ternjata laras itu adalah laras Slendro sama rata (samantara, padantara); jaitu semua sruti2-nja adalah 240 cents.

Indra Hattari of Jakarta, presently a graduate student in the Department of Economics at the University of Nebraska, offers the following translation:

> In the Music School, in order to simplify the recognition of intervals, the following units are used: cent (part); an octave, which is considered 1200 cents.

Pelog scales, European scales and Slendro scales all have the same size octave equal to 1200 cents.

When the quint [fifth] is 675 cents, it turns out to be the Pelog form with two sizes of intervals, that of the small interval of 150 cents and the large interval of 225 cents.

When the quint is 700 cents, it turns out to be the scale of European music (diatonic).

When the quint is 720 cents, it turns out to be the scale of slendro. The intervals are the same; they are all 240 cents.

The categorization given in Chart VI is somewhat unique and was not encountered elsewhere.

Some Balinese consider the pelog as being only a five-tone scale and disregard the possibility of its being derived from a seven-tone form. The following five-tone scale was given to me as being pelog: C, E, F, G, B, C in ascending order. The same musician played a slendro scale in descending order and used the approximate tones: D, C (quite flat), A, G (quite flat), E. No theoretical explanation or comparison could be offered. This same tenuousness of explanation of scales and their intervals was frequently encountered elsewhere. In so many villages there seemed to be not only a slightly different scale but also anomalies of explanation. However, in general, the pelog seemed to incorporate intervals of two greatly varying sizes: the small and the large. Each of these sizes was apt to be without uniformity.

Rhythm

One would expect that if any phase of Hindu music would have implanted itself on the music of the gamelans it would have been the wonderful, unmetered rhythmic ideas of the Tala system. This is not the case, however. Nevertheless, some very unique rhythmic devices and uses are found. The rhythms are metrical, with the main divisions and subdivisions of the music punctuated by tones from gongs of varying sizes and by other percussion instruments. The tones on which the principal accents occur are called gong-tones.

In Java, a complete slendro-pelog gamelan has seven gongs: two large and five smaller ones (which total all the tones possible in pelog). For the slendro mode one large gong is used. Some gamelans had only one large gong, but this is not considered complete. In this case the gong is often tuned to the nem or lima (either of which can be the *dong* of certain particular slendro and pelog patets) and is used for both slendro and pelog. A large gong with a "neutral" tone was found in an occasional gamelan. In Bali, frequently even the one large gong is absent from a gamelan, in which case the kempur usually functions in its place. The large gongs are used to mark the endings (finales) of the main sections of the musical forms. If the cantus should have its finales on a tone not in accord with the large gong, the gong plays the finales regardless of possible discord. The smaller gongs (kempuls) are frequently tuned to the fifth above and the fifth below the large gong, although actually one finds many different tunings. The continuous pulse between the large, primary gongs (agengs and kenongs) and the smaller, secondary gongs (kempuls) is filled by beats from small drums (ketuks). As the rhythmic pattern repeats, the ketuks may double or quadruple the number of tones played on each original beat. In one area, the music was classified by the number and type of strokes played on the ketuks rather than by a paṭet derived from certain tones.

Chart VII illustrates a simple, basic rhythmic structure common in the gamelans of both Java and Bali. An example of eight beats is given. One notices the use of the large gongs (gong agengs and kenongs) as punctuation on the finales. This is different than the use of strong pulses at the beginning of measures in Western music. Considering that the gongs have definite pitches, one is very aware of their impact on the sound of the ensemble. In the hands of skilled performers this basic rhythmic structure can be elaborated into a veritable web of tiered sound pulsations.

CHART VII

GENERAL RHYTHMIC STRUCTURE

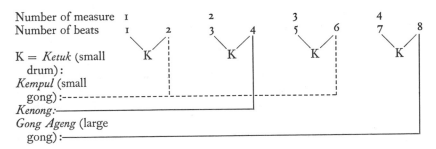

In actual practice, when more than one gong was used (ageng, kenong, and kempul), it seemed more desirable that the gongs were tuned a fifth from the gong ageng rather than to definite key-plates of the idiophone instruments. This was especially true in the villages.

When questioning IG. B. N. Pandji at Den Pesar about the great discrepancy between the pitches of the gongs and those of the other instruments in a gamelan in Bali, he explained that no large gongs of any quantity have ever been made in Bali. Most of them are brought in from Java. Most of the smaller gongs are also produced in Java. Since these are not built or tuned for any particular gamelan, their pitches do not usually coincide with those of the other instruments.

Semarang in Java has for centuries been noted as a center of fine gong manufacture. The gongs, made of specially resonant metallic alloys, are all hand beaten and tuned by ear. The deviances in pitch in the gongs seem to add a certain convoluted tonal luster to the special, delightful quality of the gamelans.

Manner of Development of the Music

Tradition has a strong hold and has established general procedures and sequences as to form and development of the music. These have apparently changed little from ancient forms. Each ceremony, dance, drama, and ritual has its own format with the texts and sequences indicating the general structure of the music. These forms do not follow those of other theoretical systems of the East but rather, in general, they employ a unique device of development and variation through stratification over repetitions of a theme or cantus. For example, the cantus is first given in long tones by one of the idiophones along with a rhythmic plan (as suggested in Chart VII). On each recurrence of the theme (or cantus), a new tonal register or a rhythmic intensification is introduced. Later new tonal color is added by instruments such as the bonangs (inverted kettles), thus stratifying the basic outline. The flexible suling (flute) or rebab supply florid embellishment. Improvisatory elaborations of a heterophonic nature develop with the music progressing in a free manner. This improvisatory quality is most important.

Modulation and Transposition

The terms "modulation" and "transposition" have been referred to by some Western writers in connection with Javanese music. The Western conception of the terms can hardly be applied to the music of the gamelans, which uses irregularly-sized intervals on instruments of fixed pitches. From discussions of these with Indonesians, one felt that these were not important factors in their music and that, in general, the Indonesian use of the terms refers more to a shift of emphasis from one principal tone to a secondary tone. C. Harajaroitsrato, director of the Konservatori Tari, Jogjakarta, Java, expressed it as being a matter of feeling more than understanding. Singers or players of instruments of variable pitch, such as the two-string rebab, often alter particular principal tones by slurring above or below them. Some did not consider this as ornamentation but called it "miring"; others spoke of it as "transposition."

Indonesian musical terminology is a constant frustration, for different meanings are assigned to the same word, and different words are applied to the same idea, by the musicians in the various communities. This is very apt to happen when continuity relies on oral transmission. Some Western musicologists have added further confusion by coining words and/or re-assigning other meanings to explain certain features. Often these have no significance to the Indonesian. Standardization and categorization have a place in theoretical systems, but care needs to be exercised that the essence of an ingenuous system is not distorted by such categorization.

Ki Sindoesawarno, in his letter of December 30, 1962, in reclarifying certain previous discussions, reflects in the following paragraph the burden of the difficulty of terminology:

> There was some confusion between Jaap Kunst and Ki Hadjar Dèwantara, the judgment of which was from Mantle Hood in his *Patet in Javanese Music*, 1954: "an erroneous inference on the part of Kunst." The "*dasar*" of Kunst means: *dang*, or dominant. The "*dasar*" of Ki Hadjar Dèwantara means: *dong*, or tonic. Both "dasars" were newly invented musical terms, and not especially Sundanese, nor Jogjanese, as supposed by Kunst and others. Whereas the discussion started from two different standpoints, it must end in an improductive "hanging in the air." Kunst's explanation itself, as starting from a non-tonic function, sometimes led to un-understandable conclusions to our musicians. For instance, he concluded that the patet Nem, slendro and pelog, was named in accordance with the "dasar" Nem. Of course he could not continue such a conclusion for the other patets, so that he left behind an amount of unsolved problems: the names of patets.

This is not an isolated case. While the problem of inconsistent terminology prevails in varying degrees throughout the Orient, it is especially acute when studying the music of Java and Bali. The specificity and accuracy of terms does not seem as important to the people as the feeling or impression that they are meant to impart.

All elements point to the ingenuous quality and conception of the music of the gamelans. In the next chapter an analysis of the measurements of scale-tones of particular gamelans will further substantiate this conclusion. Any establishment of rigid theoretical norms is foreign to the basic Indonesian concept of the gamelan. Imitation has been and still is the significant factor.

The only logical deduction to be made after all these considerations is that the idea of *duplication* is the core of the gamelan system; that the early forms of the gamelan were ingenuously evolved and the better ones were duplicated through centuries by a process that has insured artistic diversity and vitality in the music itself, not fettered by any theoretical rigidity, yet subject to the disciplines of traditional forms.

CHAPTER VI

Analysis of the Pitches of Idiophones

The idiophones, including the gongs, are classified by the local musicians according to their size (which determines the octave in which the tones sound) and the type of resonator that they have (which influences quality and dynamic level). These resonators are bamboo tubes, metal tubes, wooden troughs, or inverted kettles. The key-plate may be of wood or metal.

In analyzing the recorded pitches several important observations were noted, all of which point to the ingenuousness of this art. These included such factors as the following: Many of the single key-plates showed variation of pitch at times when the key-plate was struck in different spots. There was deviation frequently between two tones an octave apart on the same instrument. No particular interval size was characteristic, standardized, or dominant, with the possible exception of the octave and of a variable fifth which seemed to identify itself somewhat to a theoretical conception. The relationship of three fifths, considered important in some regions, did not exist in others. Few instruments had multiple intervals of consistent sizes, and this situation was evident even between the different instruments within the same gamelan. Great diversity was found in the sequence of intervals from one gamelan to another. Also, the number of key-plates was not uniform in the same type of instrument between gamelans. Consideration of each of these points will be made.

Indeterminate Pitch of Single Key-Plates

The reliance entirely on individual human judgment to shape molds, to measure amounts of metal, and to determine the amount and place of filing or beating to arrive at a satisfactory pitch is unlike Western procedure. This tends to produce instruments of many diverse pitches and tonal variants. C. Harajaroitsrato expressed to me that pitch deviants of the same tone up to 30 cents were not considered consequential. Others later confirmed this opinion. In reality, far larger deviations are common and acceptable. Quality and clarity, as well as pitch, of sound are dependent upon properly shaped and balanced key-plates, but even the best of instruments have key-plates of varying degrees of quality.

In my possession is a djubla which was made by a highly regarded gamelan maker near Klungkung, Bali. It was selected as being the best of several instruments. The first and fourth key-plates are somewhat faulty in both quality and pitch, while the others are exceptionally good. The faulty ones indicate that all parts of each single key-plate are not vibrating at the same speed, thus not producing the same pitch. This can be better understood when one considers the indefinite pitch of a drumhead. This is caused by many small "spots" or areas all vibrating at different speeds due to varying thicknesses, tension, quality, etc. Similarly, flaws in the metal or irregularities in the shape of a tuned key-plate are subject to like discrepancies.

A uniform resonance is apparently much harder to produce on a large key-plate than on a smaller one. It was not uncommon to find instruments with some lower key-plates (large) that were difficult to measure definitely as to pitch. A pelongen gamelan used at a legong performance at Den Pesar had a djegogong with a key-plate pitched at a C_3 which varied 17 cents, depending on where it was struck. The pitch of a djubla in the same gamelan was practically indeterminate on its top and bottom key-plates, which were close to an octave apart. Five key-plates on a large djago (low tones) in one of the better gamelans near Den Pesar were virtually indeterminate in pitch. One of the finest gamelans in Java at Jogjakarta had a gambung with twenty key-plates on which the pitch of five could not be distinctly established. The two lowest bars of a pelog barang gender in the same gamelan had somewhat indeterminate pitch although the logical sequence of tones from the upper register indicated these to be an approximate G sharp and E. The lowest tone of the large saron in the same gamelan was also vague. This same condition was found in many gamelans, but in most cases the overall sound of the ensemble was effective.

Western musical instruments measured by the most advanced scientific devices are found to have faulty tones. There needs to be concern when playing them. The harmonic nature of Western music makes these deviations obvious and objectionable. My own flute, made by a most reputable American flute maker and used satisfactorily in the finest orchestras in the United States, has an extremely flat fourth-space E and a D above the staff which is dead in color. Constant attention and humoring must be given to ensure satisfactory sound from these particular tones. The pitched key-plates of an idiophone cannot be treated in a like manner.

Indefinite pitch in gongs was a frequent condition, but this is easily understood when the quality factors of gong tones are considered. The prime tone (fundamental or strike tone) of a gong is generally pitched in the particular mode or scale being played. Acoustically this tone is often "clouded" by two prominent secondary tones: a high overtone which does not correspond to a lower tone in the chord of nature, and a lower tone, known as the "gong" or "hum" tone, which is very prominent. At best a low-pitched gong tone, because of so many unusual quality factors, is not perfectly clear. A slightly inferior gong or one sounding against instruments tuned in a contrasting mode or scale can easily give an illusion of indeterminate pitch. The important thing to recognize is that this condition apparently is acceptable to the Indonesian performer.

Variation between Octaves

The octave can be readily identified and is an easy interval to hear. The most elementary Western orchestra or band is taught to tune the octave

CHART VIII

VARIABILITY OF OCTAVE TONES

Instrument	Location	Number of Key-plates	Octave
Djegogong	Blabatuk	5	Bb_3—25♯:Bb_4—21♭
Djubla	Blabatuk	6	B_4—12♭:B_5—11♭
Bonang	Village in southeast Bali	10	Bb_4—12♯:Bb_5—34♯
			D_4—19♯:D_5—24♯
			Eb_4—46♯:Eb_5—39♯
			F_4—18♯:F_5—12♯
			A_5—7♯:A_6—2♯
Gangsa	Singapadu	10	$C♯_5$—18♯:$C♯_6$—20♭:$C♯_7$—35♭
			A_5—22♭:A_6—33♭:A_7—39♭
			$G♯_5$—22♭:$G♯_6$—48♭
Djegogong	Singapadu	10	$C♯_5$—11♯:$C♯_6$—23♯
			A_4—21♯:Ab_5—1♭
			$G♯_4$—16♯:$G♯_5$—7♭
			E_4—7♭:E_5—22♯
Gender	Surakarta	8	Bb_3—16♯:Bb_4—15♭
			D_4—38♯:D_5—57♯
			E_4—12♭:E_5—8♭
Gambung	Jogjakarta (Konservatori Tari)	21	A_3—?:A_4—2♯:A_5—3♯
			B_3—47♭:B_4—28♭:B_5—23♯
			$D♯_4$—27♭:$D♯_5$—48♭:$D♯_6$—14♭
			E_4—9♭:E_5—9♯:E_6—5♯
			$G♯_4$—5♯:$G♯_5$—18♯:$G♯_6$—34♯

clear, i.e., no interference beats. When measuring the octaves of the various instruments of the gamelans, discrepancies without pattern (from Western standards) continuously appeared. In a theoretical system where the harmonic feature is dominant, this could not be functional or acceptable.

The majority of the Balinese instruments of the gangsa type have five, six, or ten keys, as is the case with many of the small and middle-sized Javanese sarons and older genders. (Gender-sepuluh has ten key-plates.) The bonangs frequently have ten or twelve "kettles." The more recent large genders and gambungs have more keys, commonly twelve, thirteen, or fourteen and, more rarely, up to twenty-one. When the instrument has only a few keys, only one or two tones can be duplicated in the octave. Chart VIII lists instruments which show the degree of variability between octave tones on the same instrument. The criterion to be used for comparison in this and all succeeding charts is a Tempered tone from a scale tuned to A 440. A gamelan tone will be compared with its closest counterpart in the Tempered scale and the deviation noted in the number of cents sharp (♯), if above, or flat (♭), if below the Tempered tone.

Variation of Same Tone within a Gamelan

The use of a restricted scale requires special factors to give the music vitality and characteristic quality, though this is probably not intentionally done. The divergence of pitch on the same tone or on its octave within the same gamelan is noted in the following three tables.

A beautiful sounding smaller Barong gamelan at Singapadu in Bali showed this variation, tabulated in cents, in the gangsa and talung:

A	C♯	D	E	G♯
46♭ cents	35♭	7♭	49♭	48♭
39♭	20♭	0	7♭	22♭
33♭	11♯	29♯	4♭	7♭
22♭	18♯	37♯	0	2♭
1♭	23♯	43♯	22♯	16♯
4♯	26♯		42♯	32♯
21♯				
Gamut: 67 cents	61	50	91	80

There were some keys of indeterminate pitch on the large djegogong.

49

A Javanese gamelan heard at the Konservatori Tari in Jogjakarta had the following tone analysis for the genders, gambungs, and sarons:

A	B	D♯	E	G♯
12♭ cents	47♭	48♭	7♭	44♭
8♭	28♭	27♭	61♭	5♯
2♯	20♭	14♭	8♭	18♯
3♯	23♭	14♯	5♯	34♯
4♯	29♯	15♯	9♯	
	30♯	52♯		
	31♯			
Gamut: 16 cents	78	100	70	78

There were several tones of which an accurate pitch was difficult to establish from the tape recording.

One of the outstanding Balinese gamelans, heard in Den Pesar, offered the following variants on particular scale-tones in the gangsas, bonangs, and gongs:

B♭	D	E♭	F	A
34♭ cents	28♭	11♯	21♭	30♭
8♭	8♭	16♯	1♯	20♭
9♭	5♯	18♯	2♯	15♭
6♯	13♯	22♯	9♯	14♭
8♯	19♯	39♯	11♯	1♭
12♯	21♯	42♯	13♯	2♯
15♯	22♯	46♯		3♯
34♯	24♯	43♯		7♯
	31♯	48♯ (Large gong)		
Gamut: 68 cents	59	37	34	37

A few low djago tones recorded in indeterminate pitch. They possibly were conceived as lower octave tones of the basic scale.

The examples cited are typical of the many gamelans that were taped and measured. While the methods of manufacture of these instruments are apt to produce considerable variation, the attitude toward and acceptance of this variation strongly indicates the basic ingenuous conception.

Analysis of the Pitches of Idiophones

Relationship of the Fifths

As explained earlier, the interval of a fifth seems to be characteristic of the system, and the leading Indonesian scholars stressed the importance of the relationship of dong (principal tone) to the fifth above and to the fifth below. An analysis will now be made of this factor.

The selection of tones for the basic scale (pelog or slendro) of each gamelan follows no standard succession other than that fifths of variable sizes seem to be the only characteristic interval used in a functional manner. If one examines the chart on page 50 of a gamelan in Den Pesar, irregular-sized fifths are found. The E flat was considered as dong and B flat as dang (a fifth above). This is a large fifth as compared to the fifth from E flat (dong) down to A (dung), which is a very small fifth. The idea expressed by some of the gamelan makers that the three principal tones, the dong, the fifth above, and the fifth below, must be stable and that the other tones could vary considerably was not too closely adhered to in this gamelan. The B flat (dang) proved to be the least uniform of the five tones, while the auxiliary tone F was the most uniform.

A gamelan used for baris and legong performances at Den Pesar had the following approximate tones: F, A, B flat, C, E flat, F. F was recognized by the players as dong, and B flat, the fifth below, as dung; dang was the C, the fifth above. On the main gangsa the fifth dung (B flat) up to dong (F) was measured as being 682 cents; dong (F) up to dang (C), 735 cents. There was also a possible fifth relationship using B flat as a dong and E flat as the dung (a fifth below), but the players did not recognize this relationship. The fifth E flat to B flat at 695 cents was the closest to the fifth of 702 cents of Just intonation. It was stated that E flat was sometimes used as dong. This used the fifth of 695 cents to B flat, but the tone most closely approaching a fifth below E flat was the key-plate approximating the A, and the size of this interval was only 651 cents.

The Western conception of a fifth is simple in that our diatonic scale of seven tones within the octave permits recognition of the interval as being the number of tones removed from a reference tone. This is also possible in Javanese pelog, which has seven tones, and this approach was used to explain the interval by several musicians. In the case of slendro, with only five tones to the octave, this approach does not hold. It would seem that the "natural" sound of a fifth would be paramount in guiding the conception of size in many instances. This "natural" sound, heard as a second overtone of a fundamental, is apparent in many places in nature, such as when overblowing on a bamboo tube.

Another large gamelan near Den Pesar had the following approximate scale: E flat, F, A (low in pitch), B flat, D. The players of the various instruments recognized E flat as dong. The fifth up to B flat varied between instruments from 669 to 684 cents. The fifth from E flat down to A varied from 641 to 664 cents. Other fifth relationships possible but not considered by the players were:

1. B flat to F: 709 cents; B flat down to E flat: 681 cents.
2. A (very low) to E flat: 646 cents; A down to D: 707 cents.

An interesting situation was found in another gamelan near Den Pesar. The scale included the approximate tones F sharp, A, B flat, C, D flat, F. F was considered as dong, B flat as dung, and C as dang. The F in its octave varied considerably in each instrument and between instruments. This gamelan did not confirm the idea of stability of the three principal tones as opposed to the lack of stability in the other tones. The sharpest dong was 146 cents above the flattest. The gong was pitched at D flat (24 cents flat), which did not fit into any pattern of related fifths. The director of the group was a knowledgeable musician with some understanding of Western music. The sound of the overall ensemble was typical.

The gamelan at Singapadu in Bali had an approximate scale of D, E, G sharp, A, C sharp. There would have been a good fifth relationship from A up to E and A down to D if A had been considered the dong. But they called D the dong, A the dang (which was a fifth of 678 cents on the leader's instrument), and G sharp the dung. The G sharp to D interval varied on the instruments from 648 cents to 627 cents, small even for an Oriental fifth.

The highly characteristic old Chinese large whole tone of 231 cents, derived from the Ch'in string-length ratio of 7/8, was the basis for a fifth of 693 cents (three whole tones). This small fifth apparently had some permeating influence, for it crops up in variable size in several regions in Southeast Asia.

The preceding observations embody the salient characteristics of the other Balinese gamelans that were taped and measured.

The slendro instruments of a gamelan in Jogjakarta, Java, previously mentioned in regard to tone variation, had the following approximate scale: A, B, D sharp, E, G sharp. The fifth relationship from A to E (dong) to B was recognized by the players. On the main gender the intervals were measured as follows: A to E, 769 cents and E to B, 713 cents. These same tones on the gambung were: A to E, 705 cents and E to B, 714 cents. The size of the fifths, relatively uniform throughout the gamelan, was exceptionally large even by Western standards.

The pitches of the pelog instruments of this same gamelan were approximately F, G, A, B flat, B, D flat and E flat. These were not as constant as the

slendro tones. The fifth relationship that was recognized included the tones
E flat to B flat (dong) to F. A saron had the following measurements which
most closely approached theoretical fifths: E flat to B flat, 709 cents and B
flat to F, 675 cents. The bonangs had usable E flats and B flats but no tone
closely approximating this F.

A wayang gamelan in Surakarta had a good fifth relationship in the individual slendro instruments. The tones were approximately B flat, E flat,
F, G flat, and A, with the B flat as the bakuswara (dong) and E flat and F as
the dajaswara (dung and dang, or important tones). The wide divergence in
the pitches of these tones between the different instruments, however, made
any conclusion questionable. Changing to the pelog instruments, one found
a scale of D sharp, F (to F sharp), G sharp, A, C sharp (to D). F varied on
the different instruments from a sharp F to a flat F sharp, and C sharp from
a sharp C sharp to a flat D. The fifth possibilities of this scale included
C sharp to G sharp to D sharp, F to C sharp to G sharp, and G sharp to D
sharp to A. The principal gender had the following fifth measurements:
F to C sharp, 726 cents; C sharp to G sharp, 700 cents; and G sharp to D
sharp, 711 cents. This instrument most closely approximated the fifth
interval of theoretical systems.

The gamelan used by the Javanese gamelan class at the Konservatori
Kerawitan in Surakarta had the following approximate slendro scale: D, E,
G flat, A flat, B. The following fifths were found on one of the genders:
G flat to D, 760 cents; D to A flat, 670 cents; and E to B, 685 cents.

An interesting aspect was encountered at one of the weekly wayang
performances in Jakarta, which were always attended by large audiences.
In one segment of the wayang night the instruments of the gamelan used
only the approximate tones B, C sharp, D, and E while the singers addi-
tionally included tones approximating F and A, thus making a quint relationship possible that did not exist within the instrumental tones alone in this
portion. About an hour of this part of the actual performance was recorded,
but there was no opportunity to examine or record the instruments of the
gamelan individually.

It is noteworthy to observe that from the measurement of many key-plate
tones, fifths of many sizes were found. A few examples expressed in cents
are: 640, 666, 669, 670, 679, 685, 700, 701, 711, 726, 742, 777, etc. As mentioned before, these represent instruments of fixed pitch and not those of
variable pitch such as the suling (flute), or rebab and other strings.

Interval Size and Arrangement

Theoretical systems establish norms for interval size, thus simplifying the
process of classification, hearing, and understanding. This is true of the

Western Tempered system, in which all intervals evolve from a Tempered half step of 100 cents. The Hindu Classical system is more complex but equally clear, with the three natural intervals of pramana (comma) of 22 cents, nyuna of 70 cents, and purana of 90 cents. The combination of these intervals results in many intervals not found in Western music, yet each is derived from a determinate size and from a natural combination.

When one analyzes the intervals produced out of the scale-tones used in the gamelan music of Java and Bali and recognizes that they are the product of *duplication*, an entirely different viewpoint emerges. Intervals of regulated size as found in all theoretical systems are not here employed. Lack of uniformity of intervals between localities and scale-tone progressions of infinite variety are instead the usual. Even though no exactly patterned interval succession is followed as in highly developed theoretical systems, it is still necessary to rely on the latter as a basis for understanding of any musical outgrowth of an ingenuous nature.

The government gamelan factory, Perusahaan Gamelan Negara Nang-kunegan, in Surakarta, referred to in an earlier chapter, had a set of tuned key-plates for duplication of Barang which followed this pattern:

$$B_4 \quad C\sharp \quad E \quad F \quad B\flat \quad B_5 \quad C\sharp \quad E \quad F \quad B\flat \quad B_6 \quad C\sharp \quad E \quad F \quad B\flat \quad B_7$$
$$27\flat \quad 8\flat \quad 13\sharp \quad 49\sharp \quad 27\flat \quad 21\flat \quad 50\flat \quad 13\sharp \quad 50\sharp \quad 29\flat \quad 18\flat \quad 50\flat \quad 13\sharp \quad 50\sharp \quad 29\flat \quad 18\flat$$

This produced a sequence of the following intervals in cents: 219, 321, 136, 424, 106, 171, 363, 137, 421, 111, 168, 363, 137, 421, and 111.

At this same factory, a set of key-plates tuned to Nem showed the ensuing scale and measurements:

$$B_4 \quad E\flat \quad E \quad F\sharp \quad B\flat \quad B_5 \quad E\flat \quad E \quad F\sharp \quad B\flat \quad B_6 \quad E\flat \quad E \quad F\sharp \quad B\flat \quad B_7$$
$$17\flat \quad 18\flat \quad 12\sharp \quad 46\flat \quad 25\flat \quad 19\flat \quad 18\flat \quad 12\sharp \quad 46\flat \quad 25\flat \quad 19\flat \quad 18\flat \quad 42\sharp \quad 46\flat \quad 26\flat \quad 19\flat$$

This produced a sequence of the following intervals in cents: 399, 130, 142, 421, 106, 401, 130, 142, 421, 106, etc.

It is significant that the upper octaves are in tune by Western standards with the first. This is unusual, for most of the instruments elsewhere had octaves of considerable variation.

Another (Deagon) set of key-plates at the factory, called slendro, measured out as follows:

$$B\flat_4 \quad C \quad E\flat \quad F \quad G \quad B\flat_5 \quad C \quad E\flat \quad F \quad G \quad B\flat_6 \quad C \quad E\flat \quad F \quad G \quad B\flat_7$$
$$31\flat \quad 13\flat \quad 42\flat \quad 19\flat \quad 27\sharp \quad 48\flat \quad 13\flat \quad 46\flat \quad 19\flat \quad 26\sharp \quad 42\flat \quad 13\flat \quad 46\flat \quad 22\flat \quad 26\sharp \quad 33\flat$$

This produced a sequence of the following intervals in cents: 218, 271, 223, 246, 225, 235, 267, 227, 245, 232, 229, 267, 224, 248, 141.

In the first octave of these three sets of key-plates one finds twelve different-sized intervals and only two intervals of the same size, namely, 106 cents and 218 (219) cents. The one of 106 cents is the only interval that comes close to a Just, Tempered, or any natural theoretical interval. It is 6 cents flat of a Just half step and 6 cents sharper than the Tempered half step. Because these sets are considered superior, they are being used as reference sets. The divergence in size of intervals of the barang and nem sets ranges from 424 to 106 cents. The slendro intervals are more uniform, the variation being from 271 to 218 cents. The Javanese instruments that were measured seemed to be more uniform than the Balinese; and these just previously analyzed were better in this respect than most.

Chart IX lists the intervals of different fixed-pitched instruments of one gamelan. Flutes, rebab, and unpitched percussion are not included. The chart is developed from measurements of the instruments of a newly made gamelan of a well-known maker in a village in southeast Bali. The names of the instruments are those given by the maker, but names vary according to districts, the small gangsa sometimes being called gantung or ketjil; the middle gangsa a tjalura, penatcha, or penada, etc. The five basic tones, which approximated B flat, D, E flat, F, and A, appeared in all registers and in all instruments except the low-pitched djago, on which the A flat was most likely conceived as A, the E as F, and D flat as D. The three principal tones were B flat (dong), the fifth above (F), and the fifth below (E flat). The E_5 in the middle-sized gangsa was surely conceived as an F. An interesting deviation was the presence of an A_6 on this instrument after three tones had been omitted. The E_3 on the djago was used sparingly and at unexpected times, imparting an unusual tonal impact.

Chart IX is significant in that it gives insight into the acceptance of pitch approximations. Detailed dissection of the chart is left to the reader. He may compare the variation of pitches on a single tone, between octaves, between intervals, etc. They all point up the conception of *duplication*.

The analyses so far have been of fixed-pitch instruments. Another aspect arises when wind or stringed instruments without fixed pitch are added to the gamelan ensemble. The treatment of sulings (flutes) is very free. This instrument is made of bamboo without mechanism. The pitch depends not only on tube length and diameter of bore but also upon the size and placement of the tone holes in relationship to the blow-hole. Exactness of measurement is apparently not considered as important as in a theoretical system requiring accurate pitches and interval sizes. Placing and sizing the holes may give each flute a slightly different scale. Diameters of bamboo canes cannot be as exact as the drawn metal tube of a Western flute. Balinese and Javanese flutists admit that these instruments are not too in tune with the

CHART IX

Example of Varying Intervals of Fixed-Pitch Instruments Within a Gamelan

	$D\flat_3$	E	$A\flat$	$B\flat$	D_4	$E\flat$	F	A	$B\flat$	D_5	$E\flat$	E	F	A	$B\flat$	D_6	$E\flat$	F	A	B	D_7
Small Gangsa											16♯	1♯		15♭	8♯				13♯		
Middle Gangsa						11♯	21♭	30♭	8♭	8♭	22♯		2♯	14♭	6♯	5♯	18♯	9♯	6♭	9♭	28♭
Djubla					22♯	48♯	11♯	3♯	15♯	16♯											
Djago	3♯	24♯	25♯	34♭	19♯	46♯	18♯	7♯	39♯	24♯	39♯										
Bonang					12♯	18♯	12♯	2♯		39♯											

other instruments of the gamelan, but they feel that because of the florid, free-flowing style of their part in the ensemble the flutes fit in satisfactorily.

Most Western flutes have closed-hole keys. This does not permit the altering of a tone nearly as much as on the Indonesian bamboo flute, on which the pad of the finger acts to close the hole. The finger pad can cover different amounts of the hole, thus producing different pitches. By gradually uncovering the hole of a bamboo flute by moving the finger, I was able to vary its pitch nearly to that of the next higher open hole. On one bamboo flute this variation amounted to 220 cents. On my French-model flute,[1] I could vary an A 55 cents by shifting the finger from complete coverage of the hole to a completely open hole but closed key. A closed-hole key on a Western flute does not permit alteration of a tone. The pitch of tones on all types of flutes can be varied by the embouchure, or lip tension or placement. It is easy to vary a "short-tube" tone (the one closest to the blow hole, which utilizes a minimum of the tube length) about 90 cents. The smaller bore of the Indonesian flutes does not permit quite this much variation with the lip. Of the smaller bamboo flutes in my possession, I was able to vary a tone approximately 60 cents on a short-tube tone by changing the embouchure.

In general, the flute in the gamelan is not restricted by unison or octave playing with another instrument, but plays free, improvisatory embellishments on the cantus (main melody). Consequently, the exact pitch relationships to the other instruments is not as important as in the Western orchestra, in which unison and chord playing demand the utmost preciseness of pitch.

The two-stringed rebab, of mid-East origin, also plays free, independent improvisations on the cantus, and the players also resort to much embellishment of the individual tones, which makes the measurement of distinct pitches impossible. The fact that this instrument is played with a loose bow on strings of relatively low tension produces a tonal quality that is not as defined or focused as in Western string playing.

In some previous studies of Indonesian music, attempts have been made by scholars to categorize the scales as having characteristic interval successions and as favoring the use of certain intervals, such as minor thirds, and avoiding others, such as major thirds. The analyses given so far in this book surely indicate that definite, characteristic intervals, except for the quint, are not pertinent and that the positions of the varying large and small intervals within a scale are very fluid.

1. A French-model flute has five keys with "open holes." An open hole key consists of a ring of metal with the center open. The finger pad covers the ring and hole. If sharpening of pitch is necessary, the finger may be gradually shifted to open the hole, thereby allowing air to escape at a higher point on the tube. The other eleven keys are called "closed" and are solid.

CHART X

Western Approximation of Some Gamelan Scales

M = Major; m = minor; 1 = whole tone; 1/2 = half step; 2 = second; 3 = interval of third; 4 = interval of fourth; A = augmented; P = perfect; d = diminished.

Bali:

    Gamelan #1: F   A   B♭   C   .E♭   F. F is dong (principal tone).
                M3 1/2   1   m3   1

    Gamelan #2: E♭ F   A   B♭   D   E♭. F is dong.
                 1 M3 1/2 M3   1/2

    Gamelan #3: G♭   A   B♭   C   D♭   G♭. G♭ is dong.
                A2 1/2   1   1/2   P4

    Gamelan #4: D E   G♯   A   C♯   D. D is dong.
                 1 M3   1/2 M3   1/2

Java:

    Gamelan #1: A B   D♯   E   G♯   A. A is dajaswara (principal
                 1 M3   1/2 M3   1/2   tone).

        The bonangs of this same gamelan had the following intervals:

        A B   C   D   G♯.
          1   1/2 1   A4

    Gamelan #2: B♭   E♭ F   G♭ A   B♭. B♭ is dajaswara.
                P4   1 1/2 A2 1/2

    Gamelan #3: D E F♯ G♯ A♯   D. D is dajaswara.
                1   1   1   1   d4

    Gamelan #4: B C♯   D   E   F   B. B is dajaswara.
                1   1/2 1   1/2 A4

    Gamelan #5: D E   G♭ A♭   B   D. D is dajaswara.
                1 d3   1   A2 m3

    Gamelan #6: B C♯   E   F   B♭   B. B is dajaswara.
                1 m3 1/2 P4 1/2

    Gamelan #7: E♭ F   A   B♭   D   E♭. E♭ is dajaswara.
                1 M3 1/2 M3   1/2

    Gamelan #8: D♯ E   G♯   A   B   D♯. D♯ is dajaswara.
              1/2 M3   1/2 1   M3

    Gamelan #9: B♭   B   D♭   E   F   B♭. B♭ is dajaswara.
              1/2 d3 A2   1/2 P4

Analysis of the Pitches of Idiophones

Chart X is presented only to correct a common Western misconception about order of intervals. The scale tones of the gamelans are here loosely translated into the nearest Western Tempered notation and the resultant intervals are expressed in Western terms for Western consumption in order to clear a point. Such determinant kinds of intervals would not be a part of Indonesian thinking. Because of the restricted number of scale-tones in Indonesian music and lack of a harmonic idiom, this tonal and intervallic indeterminateness adds a color and distinction that is necessary to avoid monotony. Chart X illustrates the fact that no definite sequence of interval is followed. Again, it must be emphasized that the tones and intervals are only approximate. In reality, most of the intervals designated as major thirds are very small and are close to being minor thirds. Such a procedure as used in Chart X is frequently employed in categorizing music of primitives and can be very fallacious when interpreted in exact interval size.

Gamelans with Unmatched Instruments

All previous examples have shown a generalized scale in which five (slendro) or seven (pelog) tones are employed. Beyond the varying quint relationship of the three principal tones, there was very little more of formalization of intervallic succession. Within each gamelan there was a general matching of tones between instruments. But, on occasion, gamelans were found in which not only the gongs but also the other idiophones were apparently assembled from different sources and consequently were not tonally matched. The sound of these gamelans, while not as pleasing as the traditional "matched" sets, nevertheless had a typical quality and utility.

A large gamelan in the region of Jogjakarta, Java was one of this type. The highly ornate wooden frames, though very old, were in good condition, but it appeared that the frames for the genders and sarons had replaced earlier ones. The uniformity of frames gave a visual impression of a matched set. However, an examination of the key-plates and the resonators indicated that these had been assembled from more than one source and put into the matched frames. The pitches of the individual instruments also seemed to confirm this. The tonal quality of many of the individual instruments was good, but the ensemble sound, though characteristic, was not good as compared to most gamelans. This possibly illustrates how great a pitch divergence can be accepted.

Chart XI reveals the number of tones found on a few of the important instruments of this gamelan, which had been designated as being pelog (seven-tone). In examining the chart, one finds ten of the twelve tones of a chromatic octave instead of the expected seven tones of the pelog mode. Only tones approximating the Tempered B and D sharp were common to all

CHART XI

EXAMPLE OF A GAMELAN WITH UNMATCHED INSTRUMENTS

	B₂	E♭₃	E	A♭	A	B♭	B	C₄	D	E♭	E	F	A♭	A	B♭	B	D₅	E♭	E	F	G	A♭	A	B♭	B	E₆
Gambung	47♭	27♭	8♭	5#	4#	28♭				48♭	9#		18#	3#	23#			14♭	5#			34#	2#			
Gender						Indefinite																				
Pelog Barang						20♭	38#																			
Bonang								o	48♭	39#		6♭	12♭	8♭	31#					16♭						
Saron (middle size)										12#	34♭	10♭	4#	9#						Ind.			16#	9#		46#
Saron (large size)								15#	36#	20♭		44♭	12♭	31♭	30#		14#	24#		18♭	49#		8♭	5#	29#	

instruments. Only F sharp and C sharp were omitted. C, E, and G were found on only one. The flat D_4 of the bonang at times sounded like a C sharp. An interesting observation is that the upper octave of the bonang did not correspond to its lower octave in that some of the tones of the first octave were omitted in the second. This is a bit unusual, though it was similarly found in a few other instances.

Bonang:	C_4	D	Eb	F	A	Bb		
	o	48b	39#	10b	4#	9#		
C_5 omitted		D_5 omitted	Eb5	Indeter-minate	A	Bb	C7	
———		———	34b	tone	16#	9#	46#	

At this same place, the following explanation was given about the learning of new music by beginners. The keys of the instruments were numbered one to seven. Keys numbered from eight on were considered as octaves of the first seven. The sequence of tones for the melodies was taught by number. Although the tones varied because of the unmatched instruments, there was a definite pattern which established itself and became distinctive through repetition. These patterns seemed to have the significance, while the accuracy of pitch seemed almost immaterial.

CHAPTER VII

Conclusions

The gamelans, whose distinctive tradition is linked to great antiquity and to an ensuing long association with the resplendence of the Javanese sultanates and with ceremonies of the Balinese Temple festivals and other rituals, leads one to expect a highly evolved theoretical system. This is not the case. The viewpoints and theories of many prominent musical scholars and instrument makers, the analyses of existing tonal devices and arrangements, and the comparison of these with existing theoretical systems, all give an insight into and appraisal of the ingenuousness of this musical system with its highly unique quality. The response of the people to their music and the association of this response with their everyday philosophy is a logical synthesis.

Technically, the conception of the scale, of interval derivation, size, or quality does not correspond to or show association with any of the established or known theoretical systems. While it is ingenuous, it is not the primary, undifferentiated form of the primitive. It reflects careful artistic selection as a means for expression of the vital emotions of a pastoral people. Its quality is basically sensitive and aesthetic. Its traditions have been strictly oral. There has been no counterpart of a Bureau of Standards as established by the Chinese in 239 B.C. to set a definite criterion, or of ancient treatises such as Bharata's *Natya Sastra* and others to set forth principles as for the Indian Raga system.

The theories of the Chinese Cyclic Pentatonic, Pythagorean, Just, or Western Tempered systems are foreign to the concept of Indonesian gamelan music, which apparently evolved from duplicating that which was most beautiful or most appealing of gamelan music from generation to generation.

Many of the finest contemporary Indonesian musical scholars do not agree with the conclusions of some Western musicologists, who try to categorize, standardize, and evolve theories and terminologies which are alien to their conceptions and thinking. The majority do not accept theoretical norms. It changes the basic concept. Only in recent times have some Indonesians thought of trying to define, set values upon, or standardize elements of their music. This, no doubt, is the result of broadened contact with the West. How successful this will be and what results it will have are conjectural. One cannot predict the course of Art any more than one can categorize and define it. The art of the gamelan has been significant for many centuries.

Gamelan music is *the* accepted music of all strata of society in the cities and villages of Bali and Java. It is used on all musical levels. In the Western world the gamut between the finest classical form and folk or popular music is considerable, both emotionally and technically. This is also true in India. There the deshi or folk songs can be analyzed as being but the simple derivatives of the Raga concept. However, the differences between the deshi and higher classical forms are very great. The exquisite amorphousness of Chinese Ch'in music bears slight relationship with the raucous, popular Chinese opera music.

A universal criterion for judging these varying forms, based on only *one* of the existing musical systems, would restrict and possibly destroy an important facet of the potential artistic force in the world. To be addicted to the qualities of only one of the present systems without recognition and appreciation of the values of the others, as is common today, is depriving society of a greatly enriching aesthetic experience. Each autochthonous group expresses its aesthetic needs by different idioms and technical means. New vistas can be opened to all peoples by sharing in the artistic anomalies of music conceived along different channels. This experience will come when we *understand* strange genre rather than try to artificially categorize them according to our terms.

The hope is that the gamelans, with their scintillating, rarefied charm, can maintain their uniqueness without dilution and be ever a part of the world's artistic experience in their gentle, modest way.

Index

Index